Remembering The Gift

Remembering
The Gift

Katherine Ciolkosz

ISBN 0-9710585-0-4

In memory of my parents
Peter and Evgenija Oborski
and
lovingly dedicated to
my sons, David and Alan Ciolkosz,
my brothers and sisters,
their spouses,
and their precious children

Acknowledgements

My first thoughts turn to my family: my brothers Steve Oborski and Peter Oborski, and to my sisters Helen Tkaczuk, Mary Millerd, and Patricia Buchanan. Without you, there would be no story, there would be no book. I love you dearly. To my sons, David Michael Ciolkosz and Alan Edward Ciolkosz, may my love shine through the pages, passing on to you not only a rich sense of your heritage but also passing along a testimony of God's powerful love and strength, which are available in your own lives. To my brothers-in-law and sisters-in-law, nieces, and nephews, may you cherish the memories that have bound us together, remembering "A family's love is forever."

My deepest appreciation goes to the "angels" who came into my life just when I needed them the most: Rev. Dr. Malcolm Marler, Nancy Taylor, Elke Gagnon, Ann Maulucci, Lynn Sentner, Marilyn Pillion, and Linda Modeen. And to Rev. Robert Faulhaber, Jr., Nancy Pacht, Angela Powell, Ellen Evans, Eileen Welch and my Singles Forum friends who have stood by me so steadfastly, a heartfelt thank-you to each and every one. I am grateful, as well, for the cherished friendships formed through First Church of Christ, Congregational in Glastonbury, Connecticut, and to the Stephen Ministers and Care Team friends. You have truly become my extended family.

To Al Murray and Bob Sloan, your friendships have immeasurably enriched my life.

I wish to express my gratitude to Bob Johnson for telling me "You can do it!" right from the start. Your assistance, support, and constant encouragement made this book possible.

And to my dear friend, Ernie Clifford, I am deeply indebted for your kindness, love, and encouragement.

To Frank Simpson and Paisley Schade, thank you for your invaluable critique in reading the initial drafts and for your encouragement. To Victoria T. de Vries, thank you for taking the time in your already busy schedule to pull everything together with your excellent copy editing. And I am most especially grateful to Keith McGinnis, for your guidance and assistance throughout the publishing experience. What a tremendous help you have given me.

so fervently built our dreams upon? What can we hold on to in order to keep our dreams alive?

Remembering The Gift represents my passionate pursuit of putting all the pieces together. It is a synthesis of two stories, so intricately woven that one would not be complete without the other. The first story begins in Bosnia-Herzegovina, what was once Yugoslavia, with the memory of a separation that would last two years and would ultimately result in a journey from that country to a new life in the United States. It chronicles the return to Bosnia before the tensions began in 1991 and overwhelming fear forced hundreds of thousands of refugees to evacuate their homes in the midst of artillery gunfire — years before the spread of violence in Kosovo, and before NATO airstrikes in that country.

The personal incidents I have related are as I perceived them, and the feelings I express are mine alone. Other members of my family who also share the earliest memories may view them differently since their experiences and relationships may have filtered through differently from my own.

I was brought up with what, I believe, was a strong, traditional standard of right and wrong, doing what was expected in order to be a good person. If I did everything I was supposed to, nothing bad would happen and I was virtually guaranteed a good life. If my dreams were to be real, it was all supposed to be good.

It was not until much later in my life, during what was probably one of the hardest and most painful transitions I ever had to face, that my sense of spirituality began to change. Only then did I come to truly grasp the meaning of spiritual fulfillment and wholeness. It was a great awakening. Despite the hurdles, in the bleakest of times, faith was the substance that held everything together.

Rough times led to some major positive changes in the way I would look at life. Even I was surprised at the quiet joy and personal peace that had their genesis in a nest of turmoil.

It is not by mere coincidence but through strength summoned in the depths of despair and in the face of alcoholism, marital turbulence, and cancer diagnosed in its early stages that what evolved is a spiritual journey as well. It is an unfolding through times of separation and hardship of a greater, deeper awareness of the magnitude of God's love for us in the midst of difficulties.

Difficult times can be seen as instruments for gaining greater self-awareness. Those times can be turning points that offer us an opportunity to find new ways to deal with the changes. Ironically, such times can help us to come alive and find a greater meaning and purpose in our lives.

Remembering The Gift portrays the struggles and joy, the gentleness and strength of a family that endured time and time again. It chronicles, as well, the need we have for faith, hope, and love. It is faith that enables us not to be easily shaken, to rise above weaknesses. Hope is the essential force that keeps our dreams alive. And it is love, above all else, that can transform us.

It is my intention in relating my story to encourage and inspire people undergoing difficult times to be strong and to work through whatever difficulty they are encountering. May it truly meet someone at a point of his or her own need, whether it is at a crossroads or facing an entirely new challenge.

There is a time for everything, and a season for every activity under Heaven:

> a time to be born and a time to die,
> a time to plant and a time to uproot ...
> a time to tear down and a time to build,
> a time to weep and a time to laugh,
> a time to mourn and a time to dance ...

(Ecclesiastes 3:1-8)

Remembering The Gift

Part I

Chapter 1

Sunlight bounces off a large mirror and onto shadows on the carpet of the spacious living room of my mother's home. Unlike other occasions when my family and I have gathered, today all is silent within its walls, as if the place has fallen into a kind of slumber. Reflections of celebrations — birthdays, graduations, and most especially holidays — are all around me. Photographs carefully placed on the end tables and on the walls are all evidence — framed images of laughter, hugs, and kisses — of a family that has lived and loved together our entire lives.

Today, I am alone. As the second oldest in a family of six children, I am here to pick up mail while Mama lies in a hospital bed a few miles away. Throughout her illness, my siblings and I have each done our part to help, in one way or another, from taking care of the house to accompanying her to the countless doctors' appointments, or picking up prescriptions. Needless to say, there have been many visits and numerous phone calls to each other. These have pulled us together and strengthened our bond.

Today, there is another reason for my being here. It was something my older sister Helen had said to me only yesterday when she first made mention of the letters — tucked out of sight in an old suitcase in the basement — written between my father and mother. How could it be? For all of my thirty-six years, I had not known of its contents: letters written during a time when my father had already arrived in the

United States and my mother had been left behind in Yugo-slavia until he could send for her.

Sitting here in the quietness of this room, anticipation makes me wonder *will the suitcase still hold the letters Helen has told me about?*

Once thickly covered with dust, I have retrieved the sole piece of luggage from a dimly lit corner of the basement storage area and wiped it clean. Now, it is propped directly in front of me, a mere two feet in length, its outer surface worn. My eyes carefully study its frame as if I was to unlock an old treasure chest. With both of my hands momentarily frozen around it, I carefully lift open the cover. My eyes linger on a stack of mail tied with string several times over, the contents now exposed like shimmering gems. Postmarked from 1951 to 1953, envelope upon envelope is covered with several air mail stamps and the words *Avionom Paravion* printed in bold red. As I begin to decipher the contents of just one single sheet of thin paper, a bit tattered from Mama's constant reading of it, I catch my breath. The handwriting, now somewhat faded and stained with marks of decay, is in their native Ukrainian language.

What is so striking is the delicate, old-fashioned love story that begins to unfold as I read. My heart beating ever so rapidly, the letter is filled with such tenderness, where their souls had mingled if only briefly, if only on paper, to be read over and over again. Words spilled out onto paper their love for each other, rekindling a desire to be together again despite the fears and frustrations that had often tested their patience. Once living on opposite sides of the world, they had hungrily awaited each letter and cherished it until the next one would arrive.

Still another letter catches my attention almost immediately. Dated June 4, 1952, its yellowed onion-skin paper is masked with words tapped out on what had probably been an old manual typewriter. Reading it brings into sharper focus just how narrowly my mother, my sister Helen, my brother Steve, and I had arrived in this country. It is addressed to my father from the American Embassy in Belgrade, Yugoslavia. I smooth the wrinkles out of the faded correspondence and read:

Sir: The receipt is acknowledged of your letter of May 9, 1952 requesting the Embassy's assistance in the immigration visa case of your wife, Mrs. Evgenija Oborski, and your three minor children. The Embassy's records indicate that your wife and minor children . . . made their formal applications for immigration visas on April 18, 1952. Their applications have been tentatively approved and immigration visas will be issued to them when your wife reports that she possesses a valid Yugoslav passport and exit permits.

Since the issuance of a travel document to Yugoslav citizens is an exclusive prerogative of the Yugoslav Government, the Embassy regrets that it may not intervene in behalf of your wife and children.

The route to America was my father's dream. No one could have taken it from him. He arrived in the spring of 1951. My mother, Helen, Steve and I closely followed in 1953. I realize now, from the letters and from the stories told to me in the past, that it had been a very difficult process. Had it not been for my father's infinite persistence and had it not been for the help from others in the United States, there was a great chance that we might have been left behind.

The phone rings — once, twice, and then a third time. Intent on continuing with my newfound treasure, I am deaf to the sound. I strongly resist the impulse to answer. When it continues to ring non-stop, I jump to my feet and pick up the receiver.

"Kath ... Steve" is how he begins. There is no mistaking the distinctly familiar voice at the other end. It's my brother Steve, younger by three years. "Hey, I'm so glad I finally got you. Listen, am I going to see you at the hospital this afternoon?" he asks.

Maybe there's an urgency. I pause a few seconds, holding onto the receiver. "Yes, I was planning on going."

"I've already called the others. I think we all need to be there to talk," he says.

"She's doing better, isn't she?" *I only want to hear good news.*

"We'll talk later, okay?" is all he says and quickly hangs up the phone.

My mind momentarily fogged from the brief conversation, I leave the letters on the carpet with the resolve to go back to them later that evening.

The ride into Hartford, which ordinarily takes under fifteen minutes, now takes much longer. Heavy traffic slows me down enough so that there is ample time to think. I have been doing a lot of that lately: both thinking, and slowing down. I turn off the music blaring on the radio. Each visit to the hospital, the last week of July going into the first week of August, has left me more concerned.

Part of me is there in the car, but another part of me is thirty-four years old all over again, answering the telephone with a similar tone. It was at another time, another place, only then it had been Mama's voice at the other end.

I think back two years earlier, in 1981, when an urgent phone call had interrupted me at the law firm where I worked. It was unusual for my mother to call me there. When I had picked up the receiver, an unfamiliar marathon of weeping ensued.

"Mama? ... Mama, what's the matter?" I questioned her then, hearing only uncontrollable crying at the other end. "Mama, what's the matter?" I repeated. Still no answer. I realized I had to let her calm down. Slowly, she began to speak in such a way that I could at least begin to understand her. I could visualize her tear-filled eyes. Fear resounded in every word. She was devastated and didn't know what to do. It had been a year since her last doctor's visit. Even with her limited knowledge, she knew enough that finding a lump on her breast was something that needed a doctor's attention. It was large enough to be noticeable, and she was terrified.

I now replay that conversation over in my mind as the traffic trickles into the city. It had been during that critical time when my siblings and I were called together to be with Mama as the doctor broke the news to us. A biopsy had revealed breast cancer. What followed were numerous meetings with the surgeon to plot out a course of treatment, grueling hours of waiting following her surgery, lengthy trips for chemotherapy and months of extensive radiation treatments, all of which had drained her and caused her hair to fall out. Weight gain and certain side effects from the prescription drugs had bloated her once-average body out of proportion as well.

Throughout that time, she had fought the cancer with all her might, refusing to have it take her life. She had done everything she could to not let that happen. She remained positive and tried to care for her home as long as her strength continued. Inevitably, things began to change. Within only a year following her surgery, severe headaches came without warning, followed by a slight fever. At first the doctor insisted it was only a virus, but when her symptoms had persisted, it became time to demand further testing be done. Despite measures taken to fight the disease, we were horrified to learn the cancer had metastasized into an inoperable brain tumor. Her last option then lay with my sister Mary, pregnant with her second child, taking her on repeated trips to Memorial Sloan-Kittering in New York where new drugs kept her fervent hope alive as Mama held on. However, we watched as her energy to care for herself began to steadily fail and her condition continued to deteriorate. Deep down, she had known it as well, yet she had held on — until now.

As I arrive at Hartford Hospital and walk through the door to her private room, my family is already there with her. There is Steve and his wife; Helen and her husband and two children; my sister Mary and her husband and daughter; my brother Peter and his wife; and my sister Patricia, who was unmarried. Mama is sitting up in her bed, surrounded by several pillows. I lean over and press my cheek against her skin, kiss her, and say hello. Now completely gray following extensive chemotherapy, her hair glistens under the somewhat bright lights overhead. My brothers and sisters welcome me, and we exchange hellos and hugs. My eyes briefly focus on a beautiful framed color photograph on the nightstand. It is one of my favorite photos. Mama, wearing a dark wig, is sitting on a bench outdoors, surrounded by our entire family, all seventeen of us at that time. The photograph was taken in honor of her sixtieth birthday, attended by family and a host of neighbors.

We are her whole life, I think to myself. Ever since my father's sudden death nine years earlier, we have become closer to her. She needs us now more than ever, just as she had needed our support during the grieving years following his death. I am reminded by the photograph of how her life has always reflected what she loves above all else: her children and her grandchildren. When her health had been better, it had been a common practice to visit her at her home and find the younger grandchildren giggling and bouncing on her lap as she held them, mesmerized by their unpretentious smiles and beaming faces.

There was an innate gentleness to her. I had never heard her say a cruel or dishonest word against anyone. It was not her way, and she always expected the untainted truth from us. In our growing-up years, if she ever raised her voice or found the need to discipline us, there had to have been good reason for it. Speaking slowly, with a definite heavy accent of mixed Ukrainian and limited English, she often spoke more in Ukrainian while we responded, carefully enunciating every word in English. She had had no formal education. Our coaching, in addition to her watching television, allowed her to learn the English language at her own pace while raising six children, after immigrating to this country. To this day, she has never worked outside the home nor has she ever driven a car. She could not even read or write, except for her name. I now recall how proudly she had smiled on the day when she had first penned it.

Mama never hid behind a false image. What held steady in daily life was the strength of her faith. Even at sixty, she never questioned the source of her survival. It had not been uncommon to see her praying, rosary beads in her hands. When she had been unable to attend Mass on any given Sunday, she often prayed alone instead.

Drifting back to where I stand in the hospital room, I see how muted Mama's gentleness and warmth have become. I look over to Steve and *know* as only a sister can know. He has called us here for a reason. We are here this afternoon to try and gather more information ... while there is still time.

As we talk, Mama stresses to us: "Remember you are always a family. You stay together. Remember your father's dream for a better life for you." It had been his dream to bring us to America, leaving behind an economically weak country lacking the prosperity and prospects for development that its neighboring European countries seemed to enjoy.

"Tell us again," someone asks, "what was it like?" I nod in agreement. I want the younger ones to hear her.

As silence fills the room, Mama — the loving matriarch — entrusts her story to us, her six living children, in order that we may in turn keep the meaning of our family history alive for our children. Everyone listens intently as she begins to speak in Ukrainian, "*Dorohi moji djite.*" She pauses, realizing she must speak English in order for the grandchildren in the room, ranging in age from three to seventeen, to understand her.

"My dear children," she begins again in English (pronouncing it "chul-dren") and goes on to relate what life had been like for her growing up in Yugoslavia, hoping that her narration would leave a mark, most especially, on her grandchildren's impressionable minds. As a child, it had often been a struggle for her, a daily focus, to have enough food to eat as she lived on whatever the land provided. She continues to tell us how the conditions of the country had not changed much even to the day she, Evgenija Saljij, daughter of Dimitro and Anna Teslja Saljij, married my father, Petar Oborski. "We lived in a village called Lisnja, in Bosnia, surrounded by Serbia and Croatia. The countryside was green then, very pretty. Pretty, but poor." Bosnia, Mama had told me in the past, was one of six Republics of Yugoslavia under socialist rule back in the early 1950's. We were of Ukrainian origin, an ethnic minority in a country of then four major nationalities: Serbs, Croats, Slovenes, and Macedonians. In tracing our family lineage, we knew for certain that our paternal grandparents and great grandparents had emigrated from the shifting borders of Ukraine to Austrian Poland, or Galicia, as it was called then, and later to Yugoslavia in the early 1900's. Each succeeding generation had preserved our Ukrainian language, culture, religion, and traditions.

"Bosnia is where you were born," Mama continues, looking directly at Steve, Helen, and me. "At home." An aunt — a strong, stout woman — had helped to deliver us since there had been no doctors in the area. "That's the way it was done," she goes on to say as everyone in the room remains still.

Yes, from what she tells us it was somewhat of a miracle when a baby was born. The conditions were awful. There was no prenatal care or hospital care, and women usually worked in the fields, cultivating the soil by hand, up until giving birth. It would have been devastating, even life-threatening, to both the mother and child if complications occurred during childbirth. The village was some distance from the nearest cities of Prnjavor or Banja Luka, where the medical services were performed. It was indeed a joyous occasion when a baby did come through the delivery healthy and wailing with its very first breath. I was given the name of Katarina, after my aunt, and baptized three days later.

"It was not easy coming to America," Mama now addresses the grandchildren in the room.

"It was a year after your grandfather had arrived, in 1952, after saving enough money that he began the paperwork to bring us here," I added.

"What do you remember?" Mama turns to face Helen, Steve and me. I am quick to jump in with the first memory, my youngest memory. Vivid thoughts come back of myself as a little girl of four as I remember a simple house in an obscure village outside of Prnjavor, northwest of Sarajevo, the once-grand capitol of Bosnia.

"I remember sitting on Papa's lap, cradled in his arms, as we had waited for our family photograph to be taken," I relate, with all eyes focused on me. "I remember wearing my very best dress, although it was nothing fancy with ribbons or lace. It was Helen's before me and our cousin's before her."

"That was the day your father was leaving. He would send for us later, when he earned enough money for our journey." Mama ends, taking slower breaths now.

"I remember the boat most of all," Helen adds, going on to describe a glimpse of her recollection. Steve was only three at the time we left Yugoslavia. So he has no memory of the homeland.

In almost no time, Mama's face begins to show signs of fatigue as she lays her head back down on the pillow. Her breathing becomes labored. She takes a deep breath, exhales slowly, then another, until it begins to wear her down. My brothers, sisters, and I look at each other. There is so much more to talk about, so many questions that still need answers. We must let her rest, and agree to meet back at the house.

That evening, we reassemble at my mother's home and spend some time talking.

Before long, everyone realizes it's late.

"Sorry, Kath, but I do have to go," I hear Steve say, looking at his watch.

"Is it seven already?" adds Helen, a bit puzzled over how quickly the time has passed. "I've got to go, too, sister. We'll get together another day, when we're not so rushed. Maybe we could all have dinner first."

Everyone agrees.

We hug, say our good-byes, and they depart.

I stretch out once again on the carpet, the contents of the old suitcase strewn around me. There are other documents: a birth certificate, an official marriage record dated November 1941, and a Manifest of In-Bound Passengers list completed in New York. Some photographs rest nearby: an old passport and family portrait.

In my journal, I begin to record the events my siblings and I have talked about. What had it been like in Yugoslavia? How had we lived? What had kept my parents so faithful to each other? What had brought them here? What had sustained Mama through the trials in her own life? And what lasting impressions would she leave with me?

Faded gray images of another time, another country, another life I had all but forgotten, flood my mind as if I were intentionally placed in a time machine, carefully working the controls. I am retracing a life lived over three decades earlier. The mere thought of going back, if even only on paper, stirs up a tide of powerful unexpressed emotions. I see my life stretched out before me as an intense, riveting story of hopeful dreams, struggles, and transitions, an intricately woven personal story of our loving family meeting the challenge of living in faith and learning lessons of patience and perseverance, lessons of courage and change.

Chapter 2

It is the spring of 1951.

Quaintly nestled on the crest of a hilltop in the small village of Lisnja stood a farmhouse diminished somewhat by the surrounding thirty-five or more acres of land. Set back from a winding dirt road, the place seemed to take forever to reach from the center of town, especially when the feet became weary from walking. The old house belonged to my parents and the land to my grandparents before them. Open meadows surrounded it on one side. A small stone-lined pond nearby mirrored the sky above and more often than not clearly reflected the surroundings as a new season approached, breaking winter's monotony and transforming the scenery with a freshness of color. On the other side, beyond the fields, a lush green cloak covered the untamed stretch of land of a neighbor's farm as it came into view.

Our home contained nothing more than a small pantry, kitchen and sleeping area in one room, and a second room just for sleeping. It had a chimney, hard-packed earth floor, and six unadorned windows. On the exterior, timber was used to frame the dwelling, then a combination of mud and stone mortar dressed the house. Thatch, strongly bound, covered the roof.

The few furnishings were of a necessity rather than for any decorative purpose. We used the old wood stove for both heating and cooking. While Americans enjoyed modern technology during those post-war years, electrical power lines had not yet reached our area. From a corner of the barren living portion of the house, the glow of a small kerosene lamp cast a dim light onto its humble surroundings.

I close my eyes and picture a house without cable television and its endless range of channels to choose from, let alone any television, VCR, videos, or radio …. Since there was no plumbing in that area in those days, there was no washer or dishwasher. Doing laundry meant filling the large washtub with water drawn from the well, then heating it on the old stove. Dirty laundry was scrubbed on the knuckle-worn washboard over and over, then hung out to dry ….

Nothing was wasted, neither food nor clothing. Snippets and scraps of fabric taken from worn clothing were pieced together to serve yet another useful purpose. Beds piled high with hand-sewn, plump feather comforters kept us warm during cold winter nights when drifts of snow stacked outside the door and icicles hung from the eaves as the fierce grip of winter took hold of the land.

There were no daily newspapers or monthly magazines delivered to our door. News came from our neighbors or from those passing through on their way to town.

Lisnja was a tranquil place. Lonely, unpaved, one-lane roads scattered with boulders or deep ruts along the way made it nearly impassable for the few cars in that area. People walked from place to place. It was not unusual for us to walk a kilometer each way to church on Sunday mornings. We would follow the widened path, a meandering of footprints one after the other, clear down the hill until it merged with the main road. The somewhat symmetrical interlacing of branches in the thick stand of trees pressed close to the road on both sides gave shelter from the scorching summer sun. Whether it was an adventurous trek or otherwise, I often preferred to carry my sandals and walk barefoot in the morning shadow of the trees. Those were my only shoes until they either no longer fit or were completely worn out. In contrast, in the stark white landscape of winter with the wind rattling through bare branches, we trudged through drifts of snow, dragging our feet as the soft powdery flakes fell in clusters and melted on our tongues. It was then that the road became nearly invisible with only the sight of the leafless tree limbs heavily dusted with fresh fallen snow before us.

The church building, while large enough to hold the area neighbors, was not much more than an oversized room. An old wooden cross rested outside its only door. Shafts of sunlight coming through its six windows cast ever-changing patterns of light and shadow on the room, making it appear slightly larger. Since it had no pews or chairs, we had to stand during the Mass on Sundays and holy days. Typically characteristic of European Eastern Rite churches, a multitude of hand-painted icons worn with age adorned its walls.

Incense filled the entire church, thick enough to overpower us as the priest blessed the icons first, bowed low to the altar, and then turning to the left and to the right, blessed the people. Beautiful songs of praise came from each individual rather than from a choir. A harmony of favorite hymns transformed the rustic, old building into a place of reverence — we were on holy ground. The priest, always fully robed in long vestment attire, took his time. There was no reason to finish early or rush through the service. We were there for as long as it lasted, an hour or two at least.

Attending church was an important aspect of everyone's life, providing a place of spiritual nourishment and replenishment, sustaining us and helping us to survive. Everyone took part in worship, young and old. Set prayers were learned as soon as a child could talk, since even the children were expected to respond. When they did not, a stern look from one parent was all it took to correct the "errant" behavior.

Although our life on the farm was simple, it was also a struggle to take care of the bare necessities, food and health being the most critical. Regardless of our age, Helen and I were expected to do our share. Helen was almost seven; I had not yet turned four; and Steve, at the tender age of one, of course, was much too young to help. Starting early, we helped with the daily chores: farm animals to feed, fresh eggs to be gathered from the henhouse, or cows to be taken out to the edge of the pasture in the early morning hours and brought back to the barn at night. It was there the smell of fresh hay lingered as we carefully carried pails of milk back to the house, the creamy froth still warm from the milking.

Rich in mixed farming, our area boasted fields tall with wheat and other crops. The land sustained us. We were close to the earth, which was cultivated not with high-tech farm machinery, but rather by tilling the soil with a horse-drawn plow. At harvest time, help from neighbors or family members was always welcomed. Each season's yield of grain was taken to the local mill where it was freshly ground into enough flour needed to feed our family in many different ways. Bread was part of the daily diet and baked up crisp, several loaves at a time, in a large brick oven located directly outside the house.

We may not have had much, yet we managed with what little we had. That in itself made it special on rare occasions when there *was* butter for the Easter *paska* [bread] or when there *was* enough sugar for cookies hung on a Christmas tree. The thought of their sweetness still sets my mouth watering.

It was considered common practice to barter, or trade one item for another if we didn't have it ourselves.

The countryside was pretty then amid the grazing cattle and sweeping hills. From a distance, the trees and thatched houses created a quilt of humble tranquility. Up close, however, the sweat on the brows of the farmers could not be ignored. They labored hard, from the early hours of dawn and well after dark, doing their best to feed their families.

Entertainment was simple. There were no concert performances, no theaters or civic centers. Instead, rousing singalongs and dancing usually held in a neighboring barn were common. Springing from the heart of the community as a fitting celebration of the abundance of yet another harvest season, such times needed only an accordion and a harmonica, or *tambura*. Everyone from the area was called together for an evening of enjoyment, lasting well into the night.

The village was small enough that neighbors, even though separated by the vastness of the fields, knew each other well. Most relationships began in childhood. They would often meet at the local cafe where gossip was the favorite past-time, and rumors abounded. It was the normal place for the locals to gather when there was some free time available and their work was done. They would indulge in the luxury of a smoke, a drink, and weave a tale or two.

At home, the topic of conversation on one particular spring day in 1951 centered around my father.

"Katarina, sit still!" my mother warned, but it was hard for me. As a four-year-old, I found sitting, even on my father's lap for a rare family photograph, to be uncomfortable. Papa bent down, brushed aside my curly blonde hair as if he wanted to say something, but no words were spoken. He wrapped his arm ever so tightly around my waist as if to cradle me and rocked me in his arms for a few moments, then gently released his hold.

As my fussing stopped, I looked up, gazing at his face. For a moment, as his eyes focused on mine, he appeared worried, but the outline of his reassuring smile put me at ease. Paying no more attention to the look on his face, I thought to myself what a nice face he had.

I could sense sadness beneath the smiles. Mama had told us beforehand that my father, a young man of thirty-one years, was leaving.

"Mama, why? Where is he going? " I asked in my native language.

She paused long enough to let out a faint sigh.

"Am-e-rr-ica," she said, barely able to form the words. In a voice laced with distress as she spoke, she quickly added, "He is going to America. He will send for us *later*. We will go *later*."

I did not comprehend any of it. *Why* was he leaving? *Where* was this place called America? *How long* would it take to get there? *When* would I see him again? I was full of questions. I had no concept of time nor did I understand fully what all of it meant. Being unschooled, I had no concept, as well, of the wonders of the incredible world around me nor could I ever fathom how enormous the universe was.

Papa's destination was, indeed, the United States of America. The promised land. The land of dreams. Believing in the American dream as the way to a better life for his family, he was leaving that day, fueled by a strong determination to do whatever he could to give us a finer life. It had begun with a letter he had received sometime earlier from his older brother who was already settled in Connecticut. The letters often told of how good life in America was. "There are jobs here," his brother wrote. "Come to America."

"Let me come along, Papa," I begged him. *I'm sure I can come along.* "I could fit in your suitcase," I told him. He shrugged his shoulders and shook his head, no. I was incredulous — that was not possible. How could it be? His bleary eyes looked away. No, he had to go on his own.

And so it was that Papa left us that spring day in 1951. Eventually, he would be sending for my mother, Helen, Steve, and me, although none of us knew for certain just how long *later* would take.

Chapter 3

Papa made a home for himself in Glastonbury, then a quaint New England suburb located on the eastern banks of the Connecticut River, less than ten miles outside of Hartford. This had been well before the 1970's brought many changes due to redevelopment and well before the home construction boom in that area swelled the town's population to enormous proportions.

He worked hard as a stone mason in a construction job that paid him a decent salary, and he saved whatever earnings he could. After only a year, he had accumulated enough money that he could begin the process to send for our passage. Once my mother heard the news, the arduous preparations began. There were visas to obtain. Medical examinations and inoculation shots were called for in order to eliminate the risk of being turned away upon arrival in New York. An uncle helped with the tedious arrangements to ensure that everything necessary was done beforehand.

When complications arose in the process, it was necessary for my father to seek help through an American friend who put him in touch with a senator in Washington, D.C. His friend in Connecticut wrote this letter to the senator in early 1952:

My dear Senator:

> *Your letter of March 6, requesting the last address at which Mrs. Evgenija Oborski resided has been received. The last letter received from Evgenija Oborski was on February 17. Mr. Oborski received mail from his wife regularly each week. At Christmas time Mrs. Oborski received a letter from the state telling her to vacate her home, the home which her husband had built and that the state was taking over the place. They did not receive any money from the state. Mrs. Oborski has three children ages two, five, and eight, and Mr. Oborski does not know where she is going to live. The children's names are Steve, Katarina, and Helen. Her last address is . . . I know that you will do all within your power to get this family over here as soon as humanly possible. I am enclosing air mail stationery for a letter to the American Consul at Belgrade.*

For months, the letters went back and forth, until the problems were finally resolved. The day of our departure from Bosnia brought our grandmother, aunts, uncles, and cousins together, as well as neighbors from surrounding farms. This was a major event that everyone took part in.

A single brown suitcase, worn around its edges, was all Mama took. There were no furnishings or prized treasures to bring. She left everything of material value behind.

The ride out of the village was a bumpy one as we traveled in a horse-drawn wagon. Mama sat shoulder to shoulder on the front seat with her only brother, Vladimir, younger by a few years. Helen, Steve, and I positioned ourselves on the back floor of the open wagon, as the steady clip-clop of horse hooves sent up clouds of dust behind us. We traveled in grim silence to a train station several hours away. As we approached it, the distinct overpowering smell of diesel fuel filled the air.

"It is time," Mama said as she turned to her brother. Their eyes met, and for a brief moment they only gazed at each other. "I ... must leave you ... now."

"I know," he replied as he put down the reins that had been threaded through his fingers. "But how do we say good-bye, dear sister? How can I look at you and your beautiful children and not know if I will ever see you again?"

Her brother lingered, holding Mama's hand as long as he could, not wanting to say those difficult parting words.

"I will write to you," Mama managed to say between her tears. "I'll write as soon as we arrive," she assured him. "Good-bye, my brother. Please, please take care of yourself."

Vladimir stood up with her, reluctant to leave. "Good-bye," he said, then tenderly kissed her.

Mama tightened her grip on her only piece of luggage and took Steve by the hand while Helen and I followed.

"Good-bye, *Vuyko* [Uncle]!" I yelled out as I slipped further away. "Good-bye," I said again, this time louder. As I glanced over my shoulder to look back at him, the sight of him became smaller and smaller.

"Good-bye, Katarina. Be a good girl," I faintly heard him reply. "Good-bye, little ones."

The bustling whistle rang out, long and hard, a sure signal for us to step up and board the train. In the frenzy, Mama specifically told us not to look back. Her instructions were explicit: "go directly to your seats." I am certain she knew what she was saying; I am certain, as well, that my uncle had stayed until the train pulled away and there was no longer any trace of us in sight.

From there, the train traveled north to the town of Trieste on the Italian border to a port in Genoa, Italy. Our journey continued by boat out of the Adriatic Sea. Taking twelve days, the Italian steamship headed across the Atlantic Ocean toward America. We traveled third class since it was the most affordable. It meant our quarters were located in the enclosed lower deck, with bunks as our temporary homes. My eyes became accustomed to watching the great billowing waves of the Atlantic Ocean through the portholes of the room, enough for seasickness to set in from the constant thrashing. Since it was the least expensive way to travel, the conditions on the ship tended to be overcrowded. Toilets and washrooms were totally inadequate for the number of persons using them, with ventilation inadequate as well. When the stench became unbearable, Helen, Steve, and I would hold our noses all the tighter or run for relief when the seasickness contributed to bouts of nausea.

The four of us spoke neither Italian nor English, the most common languages on the ship. Since we could not communicate with anyone on board, we stayed pretty much to ourselves. Helen, Steve and I were always by our mother's side.

Lack of understanding created overwhelming fear, especially on one occasion when everyone had become frantic, pushing and shoving, shouting to one another in their own language. People became panic-struck trying to locate the bright orange lifejackets, then proceeded to the lifeboats being lowered into the sea. I still remember the childish fear that something was terribly wrong, yet we had no way of knowing that it was only a routine emergency drill and necessary for the journey.

Each day we walked the deck on our way to the dining hall and beheld the same sight: the glistening surface of the waves breaking in the middle of nowhere, the endless shifting of white caps and nearly undetectable sway of the ship in the ocean. In the distance, the visibility was from horizon to horizon. How vast the Atlantic Ocean seemed to a little girl just turned six.

Despite the stark accommodations, there was a great deal of excitement and anticipation about where we were going. Papa's letters had told us so much about America; our expectations were extremely high.

"What will it be like in America, Mama?" I asked one morning, excited to hear that we were approaching land.

"Your father wrote about the city and how tall the buildings are ... and cars, they are everywhere ... and you will have a good school to go to ... and, oh, so much more."

I eagerly awaited the end of the journey. Part of the reason was to see my new country, but more than that, I knew I would see my father again.

Suddenly, there was a lot of excitement rising on board. Something was happening, and we didn't want to miss it; so we proceeded to the top deck. Once on the top deck, standing up, with the railing barely touching my forehead, I glimpsed the torch of the Statue of Liberty in the distance. Within minutes, the entire copper-clad monument loomed closer, appearing larger and compellingly more beautiful, strikingly more impressive. "Look!" I shouted, pointing to the Statue. "Look!" I knew from my father's letters to us about the Statue of Liberty and about New York that we had finally arrived.

The end of the journey meant tears of relief to so many on board, especially to my mother as she held Steve, only three years old. Every few moments she glanced at Helen and me as if to reassure herself we were still with her. I held on tightly to the folds of her dress; Helen, in turn, clutched on to me.

As our ship sailed into the Upper Bay of New York Harbor with the tugboats guiding it, people on deck eagerly waited, arms waving, searching each face below in the hopes of seeing even one familiar face. Ellis Island, the "Isle of Hope, Isle of Tears." This gateway to America for so many who hoped to turn their dreams into reality marked the beginning of a new life.

May 11, 1953. A day I will never, ever, forget. Life from that point on could never be the same. Little did I suspect the unimaginable changes I would face leaving behind a rural lifestyle in an underdeveloped country for a land with so much to offer, technologically and culturally.

Upon disembarking, we were given tags to pin to our clothing in case we became separated from one another. Separation would have been easy in a crowd of what seemed like a thousand people; so the tags, which cross-referenced the information in the ship's records, were a necessary safety measure. Movement was constricted as we began moving through the line.

Helen and I became overly fidgety. After twelve days confined on board the ship with nothing but water around us and after two years of being separated from Papa, we were more than eager to him again. I had to see his face to know it was all real. I had to reassure myself he had not forgotten us. I had to know he was really there waiting for us.

My eyes wide with attention, I looked into the crowd, trying hard to remember what he looked like. I was bigger now than when he had last seen me. Would he still recognize me? I looked around again, fearful that if I hesitated too long,

I would miss seeing him in the crowd. Flushed with excitement and overwhelmed with the many faces, I glanced once more as Mama gently took my face into her hand and turned it slightly to the side. As if drawn by a large magnet pulling my eyes, I glimpsed his thin, clean-shaven face across the way. The sight of him sent my spirit skyrocketing. He had been looking directly at me, waiting for my eyes to meet his. Tall and upright, he looked much thinner than I had remembered him. His tan suit hung on his almost frail body as if it were a few sizes too large. Despite his slim appearance, he remained handsome in my eyes.

I was burning with excitement, wanting to be let loose from Mama, wanting to go as fast as I possibly could go. With one quick nod of approval, I pulled away from her, the fullness of the dress I wore carrying me as if I were floating in air, suspended with my feet never touching the ground. As I ran toward Papa, he bent down, with arms outstretched and caught me as I leaped toward him, grabbing on to his jacket sleeves, not daring to let go for even the slightest moment.

"Papa, I missed you! I missed you sooo much!" I clutched him and kissed him over and over, until he had to let go. With one long final stride, his attention diverted to Helen and then Steve. As he spread his arms wide to engulf Helen, smothering her with his embrace, my hands grabbed hold around his baggy trousers, making it nearly impossible for him to move. As Mama approached, he took Steve from her arms, hoisted him into the air, hurling and catching him mid-flight, and kissed him a number of times.

It was then time for my parents. They became totally enmeshed as Papa circled one arm around Mama's shoulders, pulling her close, clenching Steve with the other. Undimmed by their separation, her face radiated joy upon holding him in her arms once again. Then, as he put Steve down, Papa's hands fanned out and gently held Mama's face now streaked with tears of joy. Releasing his hold, he framed his fingers as to lift her chin toward him. Then, slowly, once and then a second time, Papa kissed her lips.

The long separation was finally over.

Chapter 4

A new life awaited us as we settled on Grove Street in Glastonbury, a picturesque New England town filled with pre-Revolutionary homes situated on Main Street and beyond. We were five people in a small third-floor, three-room attic apartment within walking distance of Main Street and Katz Hardware around the corner.

Having grown up in relatively poor surroundings and raised on the ethics of hard work, my parents took the modest surroundings in stride. Of course, there was never enough room. They learned to adjust and did the best they could. We children followed their lead. Everything that was old and used by someone else was still new and exciting to us.

Helen and I slept on the pullout sofa in the living room. It was a gift from another family, one of many hand-me-downs we would receive through the years. A round oak pedestal table accommodated all our meals since there was no space in the cramped kitchen. Steve slept in a crib in the one and only bedroom shared by my parents.

The turn of a small knob on the black-and-white television opened my eyes wide to a whole new world filled with images of Mickey Mouse Club Mouseketeers dancing on screen. The television became my primary source of entertainment. Its sounds, movements, and action mesmerized me. Lassie, the Ed Sullivan Show on Sunday nights, or Roy Rogers dashing off in the distance on his horse Trigger alongside his faithful Indian friend were my first tutors in learning the English language. It was mid-May. First grade would not start until early September. Summer gave me the time to learn some of the language before my walks to Academy School began.

It took weeks for me to make friends with neighborhood children who came up three flights of stairs to our inside back porch.

"Can you come outside?" one of the girls close in age asked me, slowly motioning with her hands, pointing to me, then to herself and then to the backyard. With Mama's permission, I followed my newfound friend to the bottom of the stairs and out the back door where she had brought with her the most beautiful dolls and accessories.

Shyness eventually gave way as I also learned to join in fun games to play like Hide and Seek, Red Light, and Capture the Flag for the very first time. Paper dolls, coloring books and crayons, and riding a bicycle were all new as well.

A whole new world opened up for me. How does a child describe the unmistakable thrill of watching a full screen movie at an indoor theater, eyes growing wider and larger as the characters appear? Or the thrill of rides at an amusement park for the very first time: the roller coaster, merry-go-round, and ferris wheel. Or seeing bright, colorful lights displayed in storefronts at night. Eating delicious ice cream cones: plain, chocolate covered, or with sprinkles, as well as cotton candy, hot dogs, hamburgers, and french fries. Or laughter spun from delicately applied face painting at a school fair. Spectacular fireworks launched on the Fourth of July. It was pure enchantment for me seeing a circus for the first time underneath a gigantic tent in back of Academy School. Funny clowns, dressed in a rainbow array of colors and elaborate costumes, were followed by a parade of monkeys, ferocious lions, tigers, and mammoth elephants I had never seen before. I had suddenly awakened to a child's dream of tastes and sights and sounds incredibly too wonderful to be true.

As I began first grade, my name was changed from Katarina to its American version, Katherine.

Within less than a year, our family began to grow. A fourth child, my sister Mary, was born in April of 1954. We were now a family of six, still living in a tiny three-room apartment.

Our parents were strict, religious people. Both became involved in St. John's Ukrainian Catholic Church throughout the years, my father doing the maintenance and grounds work in addition to his construction job. Since the church was directly across the street from our rental, we often tagged along with him while he worked, reluctantly helping to clean the pews and floors for Sunday worship.

"Remember where you are," Papa informed us, "you mustn't shout." I soon learned to become comfortable with the quietness of a small church with no people in it as I dusted and polished the worn wooden pews.

How Papa loved that little church and how he loved to sing. Standing in the back, near yet separate from us, he learned to carry his voice in song and prayer when there were too few men to fill it on any given Sunday morning. Mama helped by cooking and baking for church dinners and fund-raisers.

In many ways, we were a typical family. Papa was the breadwinner and caretaker. Mama was the foundation holding us together and nurturing us. Deep down, however, I knew we were not like the average American family. We were not involved in social things like dance lessons, gymnastics, or music lessons. Even events like scouting were not available to us since money was limited, as was time.

Every Sunday we attended church, knelt in prayer morning and night, respected our elders, and did the usual things good parents expected their children to do. Good behavior was non-negotiable. It was not proper for children to speak up or openly disagree. We just did what we were told.

I believed that if I behaved a certain way and was good, then nothing bad would happen and I would have a trouble-free life — guaranteed.

About a year-and-a-half after we had settled in America, and only months after Mary was born, tragedy struck our family. The news of an explosion came to us by telephone just before the local television broadcast. There had been a gas leak, and my father, working alone in a manhole at a construction site, had been badly burned on the upper part of his body, including a portion of his hands, arms, and neck. He had been rushed to the hospital and would require several extensive surgical procedures to remove dead tissue from the burned areas. The doctors then harvested donor skin from his leg, and physical therapy helped to restore mobility to his badly burned hands and elbow.

Mama managed as well as she could with four small children under the age of ten to care for. Unable to drive, she relied on others to go the long haul back and forth to Yale-New Haven Hospital, usually several times a week. Sometimes we all went. At other times, we were left with a neighbor or close friend on Grove Street.

Papa struggled through three months until he was able to return home. Even then, the recuperation took several more months before he was well enough to even attempt to go back to work. The slow process put a strain not only on him but on our entire family. The physical damage he sustained severely limited his working capacity because permanent scar tissue is more fragile to the touch and subject to heat and cold intolerance. More than that, Papa was never the same.

By early 1957, my parents had saved five hundred dollars to purchase a graceful old house beginning to show its age, complete with a maze of impenetrable shrubs in dire need of trimming, their tangled overgrowth nearly enveloping the old residence. Some of the rooms remained as they had been left — in need of painting, wallpaper peeling, outfitted sparingly with furnishings from the estate sale. With a selling price of ten thousand nine hundred dollars, it was a bargain too good to pass up. Underneath the clutter, several old salvageable items, including glassware, from the original owners became our own. It was a large home with ten rooms in all, complete with an old heating system that noisily blasted hot air through the registers in the sagging floors and carried the musty smell of the cellar throughout the rooms. At first, we felt spoiled: each of us had a bedroom of our very own.

The wooden stairs would creak as I climbed the narrow flight of steps to my upstairs bedroom, which was adorned with colorful flowered wallpaper and matching border. It was there that I often dreamed. It was my very own cozy retreat, my quiet hideaway, my oasis of calm. Two small windows veiled with translucent curtains allowed the fresh breeze to filter through as I became drawn to the sounds and scents of the outdoors. With the nasty chill of winter beginning to fade and the rebirth of spring around the corner, I would watch Mama uncover the beds of flowers as daffodils, then tulips, began to pierce through the once snow-covered ground. My bed overlooked the side yard, making it relatively easy to watch everyone coming and going.

Sprawled out on my bed, I had the perfect view of the trellis laden with fat blossoms unfurling beautiful red roses against the chainlink fence that separated our yard from the neighbor's. My father had also built an arbor to hold more pink roses Mama had planted. Within easy glimpse of my window I watched the long and shapely buds as they fully opened, spiraled upward, spread across the top, and then draped downward in need of clipping. Their fragrance captivated my imagination and set me dreaming even at the early age of ten.

In the summer, I could see Mama from the open window, wearing a simple sun dress or loose-fitting blouse and full skirt, always a scarf tied at the back of her neck to hold the pincurls in place. With a shovel in her hand, she would dig and plant. As the sunshine spilled through the trees and dappled light across the yard, zinnias sprouted alongside marigolds, daisies, and dahlias. Masses of flowers filled the side yard with a profusion of color and fragrance. The garden transformed the entire yard into a fragrant tapestry of beautiful flowers in varying sizes and shapes, spanning a brilliant range of colors beginning from late May and continuing through the end of the summer and into early October as autumn leaves tumbled to the ground.

Informal bouquets in a hodge-podge of vases added splashes of color interspersed throughout our home. A mixture of sweet-scented annuals and perennials were scattered everywhere: some potted, some freshly picked and blooming.

Quite unexpectedly, just when I had settled into the luxury of having my very own room, Papa began to seal off the upper portion of the stairway and convert the house into a two-family residence. He insisted it was needed for extra money. After the hammering stopped, that meant another move downstairs where the idea of having my own bedroom would be obsolete. Even more than that, having my own bed was all but an unknown as Helen, Mary, and I shared not only a cramped bedroom but two single beds and a tiny closet in one corner of the room for the three of us.

Mama made the most of a limited income. We all did our share to help peel the bushels of peaches and pears, the sweet and juicy tastes of summer she bought at the local fruit stand, which she would later preserve. Large stoneware crocks held fermenting pickles until it was time to devour them. Everything was home cooked; dining out was all but unknown to us.

My brother Peter was born in late 1957 and the youngest sister, Patricia, came along five years later. We became a family of eight by 1962. Suddenly even six rooms became too few.

I had often wondered how my parents were able to find the strength to go on during those hard times. Somehow they were able to endure time and time again.

Chapter 5

As the weather turned cold, I anticipated eagerly Thanksgiving and Christmas. Our holidays were filled with wonderful food baskets and gifts, an expression of kindness and generosity from people in the community we didn't even know. The sight of a huge turkey with all the trimmings was a visual delight. A large box filled with layers of chocolates — coffee creams, truffles, caramels, and coconut dreams — was like a treasure chest to Steve, Helen, and me, each of us scrambling as if in a race to choose our very favorites.

"I'm first!" Steve would shout as loud as any seven-year-old could as he tried to push me aside.

"No, I am!" I'd protest, stomping my foot, trying to get my way. "I'm bigger."

"Hey, wait just a minute!" Helen would interject, standing with her hands on her hips to make her point. "*I'm* the oldest, you know. I'm first." After all, she was almost fourteen. The teasing between us had been common, yet harmless.

"That's *not* fair," Steve would strongly rebuttal, still trying to get first grabs. "I'm a-l-w-a-y-s last." Then off he would run as Helen and I took the wrappings apart. Within seconds, her mouth and mine were bulging with the sweet perfections, our fingers sticky with streaks of the gooey dark stuff.

As we grew older, the holidays became even more special. Christmas Eve was rich in tradition. The baking of nut strudel, poppy seed bread, and an assortment of cookies began in earnest just before Christmas. More often than not, we would find Mama in the kitchen, a colorful apron tied around her waist and a bright scarf to keep her hair in place. Walking into our home filled with its luscious, unmistakable, tantalizing aromas of baking coming from the kitchen is still an intense memory from my childhood.

Mama would begin preparing the bread and cookie dough in the early morning hours just as the others were beginning to rise. "There is much to do," she would say, often letting us help as she mixed the ingredients, then stirred, tasted and mixed again.

"How much sugar?" I would ask, ready to help with a batch of her cookies.

"Just a handful," she would reply. "I don't measure. Just a handful will do — oh, two for you."

Our home would always have an extra cleaning just before the Christmas holidays. The freshness of newly waxed floors and furniture polish wafted throughout the house, while other smells — wood smoke and the scent of a newly cut pine tree ready to be decorated — added their charm.

I wondered how Mama could do it all — take care of our home, the extra work, and the children each only a few years apart — all looking for her attention. She held the family together. She did so much for us. She made sure that we behaved and obeyed. She often sat at the edge of our beds as we knelt, one by one, to say our prayers until we were completely done; early on, if we could not remember a word or two by heart, she helped us finish, then tucked us in for the night. I was convinced that she would hold a special place in Heaven some day, having raised six children and having put up with so much all those years.

The Christmas Eve meal, considered a "holy supper,"

began soon after the first star appeared in the sky. It was a non-meat meal preceded by a day of strict fasting. No wonder we delighted in all the food set before us on the table when it finally came time to eat. Our parents often told us about our old homeland. Both the hardships and pleasures they had experienced seemed part of the distant past. We heard about the traditions they had grown up with, unchanged from generation to generation.

The dinner table would be covered with a white table-cloth, often with some hay strewn on it, in remembrance of Jesus' birth in a stable where he was laid in a manger. A large white candle flickered as a reminder of the star of Bethlehem.

The meal consisted of twelve dishes. Papa began with a prayer in Ukrainian as we joined hands around the table and the little ones squirmed in their seats. After the prayer, he distributed *prosphora*, small chunks of bread that had been blessed by the priest on Sunday. He went from one family member to the next, dipping a piece of the blessed bread in honey and giving it to each one of us. "*Krestos Rozdajetsia* [Christ is born]," he would say as part of this Christmas ritual. We soon learned to respond with the traditional response, "*Slavit Yeho* [Honor Him]."

During the holidays, our house was not only full of delightful aromas, but also overflowed with people. They were a small circle of relatives and close friends who came from the same region of the old country. Some were new immigrants, who were like family since we had a shared history that bound us together. Christmas carols sung in our native language resounded merrily throughout the house. Faces beamed with rosy color, especially when a little wine made the singing more robust.

After the meal, the women usually cleared the array of

dishes, glasses, and cups, and put the food away as quickly as rosy-cheeked children gathered in the living room, drawn to the warm crackling fire stoked in the fireplace. During this time, there seemed to be less bickering or dawdling among the little ones who hoped, in their show of best behavior, to be able to open a gift or two from under the tree. The remaining gifts would be opened early the next morning.

In later years, as we became Americanized, Santa Claus dressed in his red suit and white beard often made a surprise visit.

From the oldest to the youngest infant — four generations — our family gatherings have held the threads of our family together, where the memories shared have traveled with us and bound us in love.

Chapter 6

Saturday evening during Thanksgiving weekend in 1974, Steve called me at my home in Manchester. "Come quickly!" his voice was frantic. "It's Papa!" I instantly knew something was not right and there was no time to talk. I dropped the telephone receiver in the bedroom, where I had been getting my two-year old David ready for bed, and summoned my husband from another room. Within minutes, we were all headed out into the blustery cold evening air.

As we sped along in the car, I sat bolt upright, totally silent, staring ahead through the windshield at the annoying headlights before us. I breathed a silent prayer, my mind frantically racing ahead to what I might find upon arrival at my parents' home. I played out the scene in my head as I visualized myself running out of the car, carrying David half-asleep in my arms, practically running up the concrete steps to the back entrance in the pitch-black darkness. Before I could even reach for the handle of the back door, it would swing wide open and Steve would stand there ready to fill me in as he took David from my arms. I imagined myself walking through the narrow kitchen connecting the dining room with the living room of the ranch style house, food still left on the table from dinner: perhaps a loaf of dark bread or homemade chicken soup in a pot on the stove. Proceeding into the adjoining room, I would give an enormous sigh of relief upon seeing my father sprawled out in an intoxicated stupor on the sofa. Why did his drinking problem get so out of hand?

I thought back to even before my teenaged years when the handsome father I adored began to alienate himself from the family and find comfort in a bottle. Drinking became more and more prevalent. Having worked a full day at a construction site, he often came home already unsteady, with his face flushed from the alcohol consumed on the way. I didn't think much about it, until one day for the first time, I noticed something had changed in my family. A slow invasion had taken place, and my father was the center of it.

He would make every effort to appear more sober than he actually was as he entered the living room and settled his head on the sofa pillow. When that happened, I knew I would not be speaking with him for the remainder of the night.

Papa's drinking created mounting tension for the family. A pattern developed. To protect myself from a confrontation with him, I often spent the rest of the evening behind my closed bedroom door, sometimes alone, or with one of my sisters, retreating away from the emotional trauma of the situation. I would lay in bed totally awake, half-studying and half-listening to his outbursts that were louder than the sounds coming from the television in the room nearby. Then, without fail, I would hear the cellar door slam and a knock on the bedroom door. Mama would appear distraught.

"Get up! Go. Go after him!" she would exclaim, pointing to the basement stairs, then dropping her arms helplessly by her sides. "Take the keys away from him." Usually he would cool off and listen as one of us brought him back inside. By the time I crawled into bed and pulled the covers over my shoulders, I was already sobbing, the memory of what had just happened too fresh in my mind. Normally, I cried myself into a dreamless slumber. Tears were only a temporary outlet, but the vicious cycle seemed permanent.

After consuming too much alcohol, Papa was unable to control just how much he consumed. A different side of him emerged. He suddenly turned into an unhappy, complaining man where nothing pleased him unless it followed his way of doing things. During those times, it was best to just let him sleep it off. It did no one any good to argue with him about how unreasonable his thinking was. In his intoxicated state of mind, he was beyond reasoning, stubbornly resisting any attempts to change him.

Living with an alcoholic father completely disrupted our lives. It meant not knowing how any given day would begin or end or how tomorrow would be. Some days were good, others were not. Binges were common. When Papa's temper flared, it was best to just get out of the way. On more than one occasion, we had to cancel vacation plans at the last minute. We could no longer have school friends over or make weekend plans. It meant being embarrassed at a moment's notice.

"You can't mean that he's going to my concert," I would sputter out to my mother, then almost instantly add, "like *that*?" I meant it. I was furious. One look at the redness of his face and my friends would surely know the true state of his condition.

With a somewhat sinking feeling, Mama only replied, "Your sister will drive," as if to convince herself that it would all turn out alright. It was her natural resilience surfacing as it invariably always did.

"Couldn't he think of me just this one time?" I would blurt out, all the while trying not to sound disrespectful. A part of me had the sudden urge to answer her in defense, *You can't be serious,* but I did not dare. Instead, I forced the disappointment back down inside, hoping the evening concert would indeed turn out alright.

Mama seemed to tolerate his drinking, maybe because she felt increasingly helpless. In the midst of it all, she tried to keep our home together. There was never any mention of getting help. Seeking a therapist was considered a luxury for the wealthy only. The word *divorce* was never uttered. It was as if no one knew of organizations like Alcoholics Anonymous to help families like ours. What a contrast to know that today there are professionals and organizations providing a variety of services, including specialized programs and crises hotlines tailored to inpatient and outpatient therapy to give individuals and families hope out of despair.

Taking the cue from Mama's coping skills, I learned to bear it. I learned not to argue, not to disagree. It was easier to just walk away and try to be good. Little did I know that expressing anger would not have been necessarily bad, if expressed appropriately. It is so easy to live a certain way day in and day out, year in and year out, and not even be conscious of suppressing one's emotions.

On rare occasions, I sat at the end of Papa's bed as he lay asleep, my heart loving him and hating him all at the same time. I wanted to say something that would jar him, change him, make him realize once and for all what he was doing to himself and to his family. What could I possibly say? Would it have even mattered? Hopes were high as I thought I *could* make a difference. Maybe he would stop drinking and everything would be good . . . *IF* I made good grades . . . or *IF* I behaved and did not cause any problems.

It took years before I found out none of that changed the situation no matter how hard I tried. I came to realize that neither I nor my actions would have changed his behavior.

He was the one who had to do it. He had to want to change. No matter how much I wanted it to be different, he had to take the first deliberate steps to address his alcohol dependency problem.

Over the years, alcohol had taken its toll. Unwilling to accept help from anyone and unable to handle the control it had over him, Papa lost the factory job he had held for several years after leaving the construction business. Loss of his employment consumed him. It was his only means of supporting Mama and Peter and Patricia, who were still at home; the rest of us were either married or on our own at that time. Within only weeks of being unemployed, he had slumped deeper and deeper into despair.

Now, my daydream of what I would find when we arrived at my parents' home did not match reality as the ride through the back roads from Manchester to Glastonbury loomed like eternity, maddeningly slow, as we raced against time. Tinged with irritation, every turn, every stop sign, every traffic light appeared there only to slow us down. As we pulled into the driveway, at the exact moment the car came to a standstill, I flung the door behind me wide open. Without paying much attention to anything else, I left my husband behind in a frenzy to unbuckle our son from the back seat. My heart pounded out of control in the frigid winter night as I managed to skip every other step up the flight of concrete stairs to the back entrance, unbuttoning my heavy jacket along the way. With no one there to greet me, a somberness gripped me the instant I entered the unlit dining room. As I passed through into the kitchen and then into the living room, my brothers and sisters stood with dazed looks on their faces near my mother sitting on the sofa. I braced myself for what was to follow and felt myself becoming rigid with dread.

"He's gone, Katherine," someone said from the far end of the living room.

"He's gone." Helen stopped to regain her composure. "He's . . . dead," she echoed, the words seemed lumped in her throat. Without another word, she began sobbing. My gaze wandered aimlessly outward beyond the large picture window. Helen's words had wrenched my gut. *Dead*. How could it be? The word pierced my insides like a long, sharp knife and punctured my tender heart, as if snatching every breath of life from me. The word gripped me with a cold numbness that invaded every part of my body, touching every vein, every muscle, every bone, taking with it every hope for his recovery.

I arrived too late. During the time it had taken us to go from Manchester to Glastonbury — certainly no more than a twelve-minute drive — Papa had died. By the time I arrived, the ambulance was gone. My eyes nervously scanned the room, waiting for someone to tell me it wasn't true. It couldn't be. It was all a bad nightmare I would awake from at any moment. *Somebody, anybody, please tell me it's not true.*

In the silence, an overwhelming cloud of grief draped the room, as if mocking any warmth happier occasions had ever held for our family in the past.

I walked over to my mother on the sofa, her arms crossed in front of her, her face pale, her eyes already puffy and reddened from the stream of tears. I wrapped my arm around her. Glancing at Helen again I asked, "What happened?" After a long minute, she began to speak, her voice cracking with emotion.

"He's dead, Kath. It's too late." I felt my legs weaken as

the full impact of her words sank in. The realization was too much to bear.

"No. No more. No more," I cried out in anguish, struggling to keep myself from falling apart. "No!" I roared in anger. "I don't want to hear anymore! It's not true. No, it can't be!"

But it was all too true. My handsome father, at the age of fifty-five, was gone from our lives forever.

Chapter 7

Shock, confusion, grief. Our family experienced these emotions. The shock somehow protected us from falling apart all at once. It numbed us to the point of denying reality so that we might grasp what we were dealing with a little at a time.

My father's wake was the first wake most members of my family had ever attended. Helen arrived with her husband, arm-in-arm; Steve followed with his wife; Mary followed with her husband, and I entered with mine, joined by my brother Peter, not yet seventeen. Patricia was only twelve and remained at the house with a relative.

As we walked in, supporting each other and our mother, I cringed at the prospect of facing the inevitable: an open casket with the man who had been my father for all of my twenty-seven years, now resting peacefully — his hands folded as if in prayer, holding a string of rosary beads and his small, black prayer book, its cover worn from use over the years.

Kneeling beside the casket on the velvet kneeler, I looked directly at his still face, every imperfection smoothed over with dabs of flesh-toned makeup. I wanted to cry out to him. I wanted to cry out at the top of my lungs, with every breath in me, louder and bolder than I could have ever spoken to him: *Wake up! Wake up! You need to hear me. How could you? How could you leave us? How could you go without saying good-bye?*

Where were the answers? If there were any, I certainly did not have them.

The silence became deafening. I looked at his face, from his forehead to his chin, watching for any sign that would tell me it was all untrue. Maybe I would wake up and find it was all a bad dream. Instead, a lump lodged itself deep in my throat making it hard to swallow. The words would not come out. What good would it have done? His voice lay silent. So would mine.

Nothing could quench the feeling of devastation I felt. On one hand, I suppressed emotions in the two days following Papa's death as Steve made the necessary preparations, but on the other hand Papa's death unleashed feelings related to all that had happened even prior to his death. The sadness I felt left me overwhelmed and completely exhausted.

The parlor of the funeral home was filled that evening with scores of people who had known Papa and had come to pay their last respects. Most remembered him as a kind, quiet man, involved in his little church. They remembered him as a hard worker from the early years when he had first come to this country, providing a home for his wife and six children. They remembered him as one who loved to work with his calloused hands still scarred from his accident, often with a cigar smoldering between his fingers as he carved out small wooden crosses for the stations of the cross displayed on the interior walls of St. John's Ukrainian Catholic Church. Some recalled him devoting his free time to make beautiful wooden birdhouses, lawn ornaments, picnic tables and benches or tending to repairs to the family car. Still others remembered him not as a man whose words rolled off his tongue easily but rather as one who said what he had to say matter of factly. Most people remembered his gentle side.

Grief consumed my thoughts of the alcohol abuse that had enslaved him and had caused his death.

My family tried to be there for each other throughout the funeral, comforting one another as best as we knew how. Family, friends and neighbors brought comfort and support by being with us and preparing casseroles and deserts, which they left for us at our home.

Several days after the funeral, I returned to my part-time job, still dazed with grief. I tried to concentrate on my work and seemed to be coping well under the circumstances, behaving as if everything were alright. The blunt truth was, it was *not* alright. I was only deceiving myself at the time, without realizing I was prolonging the grief process. I had to go through its varying stages at my own pace:

(1) Denial makes it hard for someone to even begin working through a loss. The denial remains until he or she is ready to deal with it, not sooner. It is there for as long as a person needs to feel it. Coming to terms with what has happened can often be a slow, painful process, requiring that one feel and express the grief in order to get through it.

(2) *Anger* is not uncommon and is a normal reaction in the grieving process. It can be directed at the person for having died or for not getting help. One may even turn the anger toward oneself.

(3) Thinking that something could have been done to prevent what happened also creates feelings of *guilt*. This can lead to *depression*, as thoughts of all that has happened surface.

(4) It is not uncommon for certain calendar days marking "what would have been" a birthday or other special occasion, to temporarily set one back emotionally. Those events undoubtedly bring back memories, which in turn may actually help in the step of *acceptance*. One needs to cherish the

memories, remember them and the person who died, and then release the person. In this way, life can go on. Accepting the reality of death often takes time and everyone has a different timetable. It is usually at this point of acceptance that one can learn to go on without the deceased person. That does not mean the deceased person is forgotten or no longer loved.

(5) The worst thing someone can say is "I know how you must be feeling." No one can really even begin to comprehend the full range of emotions involved unless they themselves have had a similar experience. This is where *empathy* plays a major role.

(6) In my own grieving process, I have found that different phases of mourning may overlap one another until, at last, the process has worked itself through. At that point, there is generally *peace*.

Mama took my father's untimely death the hardest. He had been her whole life. She mourned him, as tradition taught her, for one year in solemn dark clothing. Her eyes often betrayed the sadness within her and left an impression of how difficult it was for her to go on without him. In time, she did begin to let go, all the while resigned to the fact she would never re-marry. Eventually, the passing years subdued her grief as she faced the realities of her life with acceptance and faith in her solo journey.

Chapter 8

After my father's death, no matter how much I may have thought I was prepared to someday also lose my mother, in reality I was not prepared at all.

I did not know much about the signs of approaching death. I just sensed it. Acting on intuition had never been easy for me, yet somehow I knew what the right thing to do was. One of God's gifts, intuition nudges us and stays with us until we respond.

It is now August 7, 1983. My attention is diverted to the final arrangements of a friend's bridal shower. Exhausted at the end of the day, I wonder whether I have the energy to make the fifteen-minute drive from Glastonbury to Hartford Hospital. *After all,* I rationalize, *I can go the next day.* My siblings and I had all been with Mama yesterday, when Steve had called us all together. Remarkably, her condition has improved somewhat, and the doctors would be discharging her in a day or two, even if it meant the portable oxygen tank would go with her. Something, however, tells me to leave things at home and go to her. I cannot explain the deep inner stirring that tugs at me. I only know how strong it is. The feeling persists until I know I have to be there with her.

As I approach her lying still in bed, several pillows cushioning her head, I lean over, press my cheek against her translucent skin, and kiss her. "I'm here, Mama," I whisper, pushing aside a few stray strands of hair from her forehead. Her eyes open and she looks up at me, taking my hand into hers, squeezing it. We are alone. That in itself is particularly unusual for a Sunday evening. Ordinarily, every spare space in the room would have been taken as the family gathered to see her. This evening, no one happens to be around since many of them had stopped by earlier in the day.

She and I spend the hour undisturbed, hand-in-hand, as I pull myself up to be closer to her. I recall a much earlier time, as a little girl, perhaps seven or eight. I turn the memory over in my mind, a time when I would sit beside her on the living room sofa as she brushed and braided my hair. I would wear a pretty party dress and a white bow rested at the end of each braid. The birthday party I would be going to was the perfect time to wear my new white socks with my black patent leather shoes. After all, Mama had said they were only for special occasions.

Now, I bask in the joy of being able to be alone with her. It is as if we need the time together, she and I, special time God has allowed for only the two of us.

Words do not have to tell me that she loves me. The feeling is there. I just know it, and she knows how much I look up to her and love her. Saying "I love you" had never been expressed in my growing-up years. I could not recall ever hearing it from either parent. It had not been until during the nine years after my father's death when I had become closer to my mother, that she expressed it openly and I to her. How ironic that those very words of affection often remain unspoken, as if people wait for the right time to say them.

Laughter mingles with tears as she and I reminisce about the twists and turns of our lives. I am in my early thirties now,

married, with two young sons. She is both mother and con-
fidante as we talk freely about the things that matter: husband,
home, children, family, friends. In many ways, I find myself
mirrored in her. Certainly, I have inherited her eyes, the curve
of her nose. More than that, I love family gatherings and a
house full of friends.

My head quickly fills with images of the fun times we had
had together as a family: summer barbecues in her backyard;
a special wedding shower for Helen and the part I had taken
as a bridesmaid at her wedding. There had been countless
birthday parties; every month seemed to have had a member
of the family's birthday marked on it. Most especially, I
remembered holidays at Mama's home. Each time we had
gathered, it had been a time to catch up on our lives and stay
closely connected. She brightened for a moment at the recollections of some of the unforgettable times.

Sitting beside Mama now, she looks over at me and
quickly detects from our conversation, though, that all is not
as wonderful as I often portrayed on the surface.

"What is it?" she asks. "What is troubling you?"

She knows me so well, I think. *She knows how I tend to see
things not always as they are but as I wish they would be. She does
not know, though, that I realize things will never be the same.*

"There is so much I don't understand," I replied.

"Tell me what you mean," she said.

"There is so much I wish were different. Why must some
things turn out the way they do?"

"The answers are not always there; sometimes it takes
time to find what you are looking for."

Yes, I was looking for easy answers, wanting so much for
her to tell me the "secret" to life, as if some magical word from
her would make sense of everything.

"You just have to do your best and go on," I heard her say. "Your faith is put to the test every day. But you must believe that God will provide a way. Remember no matter what that you are special. Just as your brothers and sisters are special. Just as our family is special. And that you have each other."

As we talk more, I think *what will I do if I lose Mama, too?*

She looks at me straight in the eyes as if she could see right through me. "You must go on."

I adjust her pillow and hold her wrinkled hands in mine a little longer. Her eyes, once full of vibrance, begin to close more often than they remain open. She is tired. It is time to let her rest, yet I find it takes tremendous effort to leave her. *Why? Why does it feel like I have to pull myself away from her? Why is it so hard to go?* She is scheduled to come home in a day or two.

I slowly slip off the bed, straighten out the light covers, and bend over to gently plant a kiss on her cheek, removing my hand from hers. I begin the short distance to the door out of her room, but something nudges me to go back. *Could it be? A subtle whisper of an angel in gossamer wings: "Go back to her. Go back and give her one more kiss."*

Mama's eyes are closed as if the medication has placed her into a deep sleep for the night. I touch her soft face and kiss her one last time, feeling her warm tender breath against my cheek. As I walk to the door, I slowly glance back. A peacefulness lies over her. I stand there for only a moment, blinking back the tears. So softly as to be barely audible, I whisper, "Good-bye, Mama," and slowly close the door.

She wanted more than anything to be home, to be near what meant the most to her. As was her wish, less than two days later, she left the hospital with the understanding that someone would be with her at all times. Once home, arm in arm with Steve's wife Debbie alongside her, they were able to walk around the beautifully blooming perennials she had so faithfully tended in the past.

Her gardens were much more than plants. They provided endless hours of pleasure as she had often worked the soil and watched them bloom, fulfilling her and invariably lifting her spirits. Her soul thrived in their beauty. As her health had begun to decline, she often sat on an old wooden bench in summer's late day radiance, gathering comfort from the beauty around her.

Now home from the hospital and completely tired from walking around the boundaries of her yard, she made her way inside so she could rest.

That very afternoon, only a few hours after coming home, Mama collapsed and died. I never had the chance to talk with her again after the hospital visit. There is no doubt in my mind that our time together was God's grace working in our lives, allowing us the time alone to talk about our lives and say what needed to be said, and most of all, to say "I love you" one last time.

The very best gifts my mother could have ever given to me are not wrapped in paper or tied with colorful ribbons. Her priceless gifts are her warmth, her strength, her reverent spirit and her determination to survive despite times of despair, pain, and sorrow. Surely, her faith had been tried on all too many occasions, yet she was able to turn weakness into strength and sorrow into the joy she found in her family and friends.

On the day of her funeral, an incredible peace transcended the grief of her passing and filled the little Ukrainian Catholic Church. There was an unexplainable feeling that she is in a better place, her struggles now ended. To my utter amazement, I began singing some of her favorite Ukrainian hymns during the funeral mass, clutching a tissue in one hand and holding on to one of my sisters with the other.

Chapter 9

"**M**ary, I've been thinking," I said to my sister, several months after Mama's death. "Have you ever thought about traveling to Yugoslavia, back to the land of our roots?" The thought filled me with both apprehension and excitement.

"Oh, yes, Kath! I've been thinking the same thought! It's been on my mind for some time. I'd love to see all the people and places Mama and Papa talked about so much!" she replied eagerly.

More than anything, I knew I wanted to see Uncle Vladimir, who had driven my mother, Helen, Steve, and me to the train station so many years before. I wanted to hear his story of that eventful day and all the days since then. For Mary, it was a nostalgic yearning for a place she had never seen yet one she had heard so much about.

"We could visit Mama's four sisters as well." My father had left behind only a brother, who lived in Vukovar. Besides that, there were more than a dozen cousins we had never met yet had heard about in the letters my parents had received over the years.

I have never been on an airplane before; so the thought of flying over the ocean for six or seven hours both terrified and thrilled me. Fear of flying, fear of the ocean, take over. *Oh, no. I can't do it.* (Perhaps the fears stemmed from my childhood memory of looking out of the ship's portholes into the vast ocean, as we were making our journey to New York harbor.)

Somehow, a sense of calm settled on me just as Mama's words used to calm me. It was as if her gentle spirit had returned to remind me to trust it will be alright. I realized the trip would be a risk worth taking; it was something I *had* to do. The next step was to begin making the necessary travel plans. Excitement soon overcame any anxieties I had previously had.

Finally, in September of 1984, a little over a year after Mama's death, I began my journey back to my roots.

Mary and I traveled from Kennedy Airport in New York to Zagreb, Yugoslavia, then on to Belgrade.

Getting off the Yugoslavian airplane, we were greeted by uniformed military personnel throughout the airport. Though dignified looking in their dark green uniforms with sashes tightly crisscrossing against their upper bodies, their presence intimidated Mary and me as they walked stiff-legged past us cradling their rifles across their chest. Others stood rigidly at attention at main terminal exits, averting any eye contact whatsoever.

An older man, an official, motioned for us to follow him.

"*Zdravo*," he said in the Serbo-Croatian language.

"'Hello', he said," I whisper to Mary as he motioned to see our passports. He seemed to scrutinize mine in particular, especially noting my place of birth was listed as Yugoslavia. He lifted his eyebrows, surprised, then conferred with another worker standing nearby. Obviously annoyed, they quickly shook their heads, enough to solicit an onslaught of penetrating stares from others in the airport. As I looked directly at him, I breathed a sigh of relief when he finally stamped the passport and waved us on.

"*Hajde,*" he said with a stoic restraint in his words, his eyes continuing to gauge my comprehension. He repeated, "*Hajde. Go.*"

Mary and I picked up our heavy luggage and laboriously slipped through the gate, all the while turning our heads and shoulders every so often and watching for the slightest clue that something might be wrong. (I had heard accounts of the economic failures and internal political differences taking place, but little did I know at the time that the ethnic hostility was brewing in Yugoslavia.) Our baggage went through a thorough check, and finally, the inspection was over. What a relief!

Instantly, our attention focused on a group of five people standing behind the glass doors of the terminal guarded by the soldiers with guns. My eyes were immediately drawn to a thin man in the middle wearing a cap, waving furiously with both arms, trying to get our attention. *Could it be? Could it be Uncle Vladimir?* The vision of him, after our thirty-one years apart, is incredible — too wonderful — to believe. *Yes, it is him! I know it is!* He resembled my mother so closely, there was no doubt. He had traveled from his eighty-acre farm — a trip taking four hours by automobile — in order to meet us. I returned his wide smile only long enough to put down the luggage and stretch out my arms to embrace him.

"*Vuyko!*" I exclaimed. "It is so good to see you, again!"

"*Katarina!*" he shouted, tears running down his cheeks, as he pulled me close to him. In a flurry of excitement, I gently released him long enough to introduce him to Mary, whom he had never met.

My eyes focused on the other four persons, trying to

remember who each one might be. To one side stood a woman of medium height and build; she couldn't have been more than in her early 70's. Almost instantly, there was something magnetic about her. Her kind face and quiet manner reminded me so much of my mother. *It must be Mama's sister, Katarina.* The identical smile brightened up her face, flashing a gold tooth, just as my mother had when she had first arrived in the United States. A dark kerchief covered her head as was the custom especially among the older women. Her shapeless brown dress was simple, unlike that of others at the airport who were wearing brightly colored blouses lavished with hand-stitched, detailed embroidery.

My cousin Genjo [Aunt Katarina's son], a handsome man, sturdy, broad-shouldered with wavy dark hair streaked with traces of gray, greeted us warmly. Seeing his boyish grin, I was speechless, meeting him for the first time. The letters he had often sent us after Mama's death told us of how he and his wife worked in the government fields, often under the hot summer sun, from 6:00 a.m. until 6:00 p.m. for very low wages. His wife, Stefka, a slender, sparkling-eyed woman, her hair pulled in a bun on top of her head, stood beside him, her smile cast a soft warm glow to her face as she raised her arms to embrace us.

Practically bumping shoulders with Genjo was another uncle, who lived only an hour from the airport. His wife, Mama's sister Hanja, now a semi-invalid due to recurring heart problems, had asked him to greet us in her place. Mary and I would be visting her home first, although Genjo would be our guide for the majority of our three weeks' stay.

Jet lag and the international time difference played havoc on both our minds and bodies. Mary and I adjusted our watches ahead six hours and noticed it had taken a total of seventeen hours to travel from Connecticut to our destination. Though exhausted, she and I were consumed with sheer excitement. Eager to speak with each of them, we did not want to waste a minute in getting to know them and learning about their lives. We had so much to talk about, so much to do in such a short time.

Stepping out of the airport, I felt as if I were placed in a time warp. Not much had changed in the thirty-one years since I had left the country. As we drove out of Belgrade, farther away from the city, black smoke curled into the sky from the few factories we passed along the way. The glow of morning sunshine filled the fields of corn stretched endlessly on either side of the highway. We passed villages that seemed unchanged. From the window of Genjo's small automobile, primitive homes came into view with cream-colored brickwork, their roofs covered with red clay tiles. Some had front gardens and gates defining each property. Modern improvements had been slow to reach the area. The simple natural setting augmented by the sight of villagers, walking or riding bicycles, of small cars yielding to horse-drawn wagons competing in the flow of traffic, all captured the ambience of a time technology has almost forgotten.

As we approached the town of Sremska Mitrovica, the smells changed drastically. Even before the chickens, livestock and pigs came into view, the barnyard smells made our noses twitch. I suspected that the drainage systems were not adequate. In the late September sun, it took a major effort for Mary and me to appear unaffected by the foul air.

We entered Aunt Hanja's home, immediately noticing objects of faith surrounding us: a crucifix on one wall, a painting of the Last Supper on another, an icon draped with a hand-embroidered cloth on yet another wall. It did not take long for Genjo, his shirt sleeves rolled up, to open a bottle of homemade plum brandy called *slivovitz.*

"*Nah Zdorovja* [To your health]," Genjo declared a customary toast, as he raised his glass high and as we lifted ours in unison. "To your health," I repeated in response. *To life.*

Several neighboring women helped to prepare dinner, serve, and clean up. Eating and drinking became the focus for the rest of the day as everyone crammed their chairs around a single table underneath an arbor outdoors. We feasted on bowls of hearty homemade chicken soup, fresh salad, and platters of fresh chicken and pork placed before us on a vintage hand-embroidered tablecloth. Genjo opened yet another bottle as we broke round loaves of freshly baked breads. The women continued serving and took delight in watching as hearty appetites were richly satisfied. "Eat. You must eat!"

Communication was a bit awkward at first since they knew no English and my Ukrainian was somewhat limited. The important thing, however, was that we *were able* to converse, sometimes with the harmonious blend of chuckles followed by bursts of spontaneous roaring laughter, especially when I struggled for the right word to use or attempted to get the message across in a round-about way.

Later that afternoon, Mary and I unpacked our overstuffed bags. Everyone held their breath, seemingly in awe of all the gifts we brought: blue jeans, sneakers, work clothes, and for the little ones, miniature dolls and small trucks. Simple gifts like ground coffee, drinking straws, bandaids, or packages of Kool-Aid, so common to Americans, were eagerly received since these food and clothing items were either scarce or just too expensive for them to buy. It became apparent from their expression that our relatives felt they had little to give us in return.

What they did give us during our stay, however, could not be measured in material terms. A simple, hard-working people, with no microwaves, no expensive cars, no large homes, they nevertheless overflowed with abundant hospitality and boundless love. Unfailingly polite, they adopted Mary and me as their own and could not do enough for us. Everywhere we traveled, we were presented with special meals prepared of favorite foods we love. Without fail, they brought out the homemade wine or plum brandy and encouraged us at each meal to have as much as we wanted. *Too much drinking,* I thought. (I soon learned that alcohol consumption was an integral part of their social tradition. Nondrinkers were relatively rare.) After the meals, strong coffee was served in demitasse cups as we leisurely sat around the dinner table. There was joyous singing of festive songs my parents once sang. Unhurried conversation often lasted for hours, sometimes lingering until the day slipped into night and the night went unnoticed into early dawn.

Each day of our visit was filled with trips to meet another aunt or cousin we had not known existed. Yet another lovingly prepared meal was presented to us. Some of the younger ones had some knowledge of the English language, which was taught in their schools. As a result, our communication became that much easier. We now had interpreters to help us.

Though thousands of miles apart, literally and figuratively, we shared a mutual love. I dreaded the time we would have to say good-bye.

One of the special highlights of the trip for me was traveling south about four hours by car outside Belgrade into Bosnia, back to the place of my birth. A long time had passed since I last traveled the back roads of my native village, where the eye could see the rugged beauty of the land for miles and miles and where the sight of cattle grazing in pastures and sheep meandering were all too common. Flatlands now gave way to steep roads, rounded peaks descended to pastoral farmlands, and ascended around mountains, until we came upon Lisnja just beyond the town limits. An incredible feeling of awe filled me as we passed through the village and beyond the small local café, tobacco smoke emanating from its open door.

Leaving Genjo's car a short distance from Uncle Vladimir's farm, my feet trod the old familiar dirt road and passed the family graveyard. Standing in the shadow of grass unintentionally left to grow at least knee-deep not due to lack of respect for the dead but more due to lack of time, was an old wooden cross marking the grave of Grandmother Saljij. In the center was her name carved by hand. Near it, another cross, much smaller in size, framed the two weathered pieces of wood nailed together, marking the burial ground of an infant.

"It is your mother's first child," Uncle Vladimir said solemnly, raising his two fingers to frame his chin and going on to tell Mary and me about the baby who had been born before Helen. The child had not even had a chance. Conceived during the height of World War II under unimaginable impoverished conditions and during a time of severe draught, it died at birth.

"I know," I softly answered my uncle. Mary and I both knew. We remembered how hard it had been for Mama to talk about it; how she had refused to elaborate. God must have needed another angel, Mama had told us, as if to make any sense of the loss she bore.

We climbed back into Genjo's automobile, made a turn, and traveled up another unmarked, isolated road only a short distance away. I eagerly searched the surroundings, each moment bringing me closer to a familiarity I once knew, almost certain the road would lead us to the old farmhouse. Angling the bend, we passed a farmer diligently at work in his field. He looked up to wave, then paused in his plowing to answer Uncle's neighborly greeting. Instantly, in the distance an unfamiliar house came into view, much too large to be the home I had been born in. I soon discovered that the old place I remembered had been razed. In its spot was a newer two-story brick dwelling overlooking the road. The barn and outbuilding remained untouched. To the side, I recognized the rustic grain storage shed, etched by time and weathered to a pale gray over the years. As if in a dream, the musty sweetness within the timeworn structure brought on flashbacks of times I had played in it with Helen and Steve as a child. A stately tree nearby, once the very spot where our photographs were taken the day of our departure in 1953, was a landmark from another old photograph I was carrying with me.

The new homeowners came out to greet us as we got out of Genjo's car and eased into animated conversation. It was emotional when a certain elderly neighbor, bent over with age and balancing his weight on his wooden cane, came up the dirt road shortly after our arrival. News of "the Americans" in Lisnja had spread. Quite alert for his seventy-plus years, he poured out his recollections as a witness to the past, his eyes immediately lighting up when asked to tell us what he remembered. We were eager to hear his words spill out. His version of our departure in 1953 intrigued me and I listened even more carefully, mindful that I was at the very spot where it had all begun for me. The memory of that moment is forever etched in my heart. I had no words to adequately express the depth of emotion it stirred in me.

As the days of our visit pass, we heard about members of the younger generation of our family who had left the area rather than follow in their parents' footsteps of working the land. Encouraged to seek employment in industrial areas of Western Europe, some had chosen to live in Germany, Austria, or Switzerland in order to provide a better living for their own families.

Genjo asked Mary and me to respect the restrictions imposed by the Yugoslavian government to outsiders. That meant avoiding any criticism of the country's politics or of their way of life. He cautioned us against photographing the people or buildings without permission. As we traveled, the distinctive characteristics of the region, the people, food and dress became more and more clear. In the cities, we found the younger generation influenced by the western culture. In the villages, it was as if time had stood still. Old folk traditions remained an integral part of everyday life.

With each passing day, our time together became a celebration embodying a spirit of another sort: a celebration of a family worlds apart, now reunited. On the day before we were to return to the United States, Genjo called his neighbors and other family members together. It was a time to dance. We held hands, first as couples, then in a light-stepping circular dance, singing along and swaying to the music as dusk approached, without a thought of what the next day would bring. It was our last night together.

The next morning, we rose early and packed our luggage in Genjo's car. The mid-October sun stretched across the highway as we made our way to the Belgrade airport. Heavy silence filled the car. This was the most grueling part of our trip, for it worked on all of my emotions — far beyond mere words. I realized I would probably never see any of these dear loved ones again. I grasped to take everything in, absorbed in every moment. Aunt Katarina clung to Mary and me in the back seat, holding our hands tightly as she glanced intently at our faces. Her eyes, slightly moist, hovered on the verge of tears. I wanted to tell her what seeing her had meant to me. I wanted to tell her I would never, ever forget her outpouring of love. As for Uncle Vladimir, I would never forget his sharing of memories. With the familiar dread of saying good-bye, I wanted to tell them I would always remember them.

At the airport, in a bittersweet moment, I wrapped my arms to embrace each relative who had seen us off. With heads lowered, we were unable to voice parting words and, instead, shed tears as we held one another close one last time. With Aunt Katarina close, I looked into her eyes once so bright with excitement at our coming, now filled with sadness at our leaving.

The announcement came across, first in Serbo-Croatian then in English, "May I have your attention, please. We are now ready to begin boarding Yugoslav Airlines Flight 502 to Zagreb and then on to New York."

Mary and I were quickly drawn into the line of passengers ready to board the flight, and as I turned my head with a backward glance one last time, I could only see Uncle Vladimir standing in front of the others, the pain of parting clearly visible on his face. With a brisk movement of my hand, I waved a final good-bye.

∾

Over a decade has passed since my trip to Yugoslavia. All too many aunts and uncles have since passed away. I have left behind the people, but in my heart I have carried home a glimpse of their caring personalities and their way of life, expressed not only in their genuine hospitality but also in their boundless love. One of the last words Genjo had spoken were vows to stay in touch. I later learned that I could telephone Yugoslavia directly at a cost of only about a dollar a minute. We have kept in touch through our letters, our care packages, our telephone calls on Christmas and Easter. Their consistent replies, although difficult to decipher at times, have kept our families united.

Today, so much of what was once Yugoslavia has been severely hit and the beautiful green countryside I remember stands as a nightmare landscape of destruction, nothing more than a mere shadow of its former self.

All of these events make me wonder. I marvel at the way God works the tapestry of events and experiences of our lives into the person we become. How different my life would have been had my parents not settled in the United States. That very thought helps me to appreciate so much. Above all else, I appreciate being alive in this great land.

My parents held tight to the American dream. Separation was not easy. Neither was raising a large family on a limited income. There were many trials, no doubt, and their patience had been tested to the limit. In the midst of it all, we were sustained. Each time, we learned to go on.

By far, America is a great nation. Despite its problems, its differences, this country is unlike any other.

Part II

Chapter 10

Sometimes, we live life or look at it as if we are wearing rose-colored glasses. For me, it seemed that way. Growing up in a childhood where things could have been better empowered me to try to make my future more favorable. I wanted more than anything to have a good life, free from the turmoil I had experienced in the past.

Growing up in a home with an alcoholic parent influenced me in such a way that I did *not* want to repeat a similar behavior. I refused to follow in those same steps. Alcohol would *not* be a crutch for me in dealing with stress or unhappiness. Quite often in life, the exact opposite happens. A parent's influence can be so damaging that it is enough to make a person wallow in despair, unable to stop drinking apart from some type of help for recovery. Without help, the pattern continues until the cycle of abuse is broken. For me, thank God, the taste of trauma was enough to make me run from alcohol as a solution.

After I graduated from high school, my parents encouraged me to seek employment in order to support myself. If I wanted to further my education, I had to do it entirely on my own. I began by signing up at one of the local universities, hoping to take one class a semester while I worked full-time.

Instead of continuing college, I began dating a boy I had met in high school. He was beginning his second year in the Army. We kept in touch by letter or phone call and dated when he came home on leave. News of Vietnam brought fear;

relief came with news he was being shipped to South Korea. He and I had everything in common, or so it seemed. It was as though I could relate to his upbringing and he to mine. Upon his discharge a few years later, I felt content with the course our relationship was taking.

When we married in 1969, I felt even more certain that our relationship would last forever. As a naïve twenty-two-year-old, I dreamed of the happiness I would find in a loving partner and a beautiful home. Three years into the marriage, ecstatic with the news I was pregnant, I visualized the happiness that would surely follow.

The birth of my sons, David in 1972 and Alan in 1978, brought an incredible joy into my life. Holding each of my sons in my arms only moments after giving birth filled an emptiness and opened my eyes to the wonderful miracle of life. I took on the role of "Super Mom," trying to keep up with my boys' irrepressible energy and unending curiosity, working part-time and trying to do all that needed to be done. It was easy to focus on the needs and wants of a husband and children. They always came first. My days often closed with my reading to my sons their favorite bedtime stories, tucking them in, and then turning out the light as I ended with "Sweet dreams. I love you." At the heart of my earnest attempts was the desire to keep our home a place of nurture for our children and to help them grow into responsible adults, even in a world filled with a false sense of values.

Their growing-up years were frequently marked by well-planned birthday parties and sleepovers. Our family gatherings often totaled well over twenty people as my brothers and sisters were now married and had children of their own. It became a challenge to accommodate everyone at our sit-down dinners, especially Christmas Eve. As my sons became older, there were soccer meets during the summer, ice hockey games in the winter months to break winter's monotony, and middle school band concerts and field trips. While the activities were sometimes enough to frazzle the best-intentioned parent, those were wonderful fun times. We were also blessed with good friends. All in all, my husband and I appeared to be the perfect couple. We appeared to be the perfect family.

In striving to live a better life, I had learned to overlook the not-so-good things from an early age. During my marriage of over twenty-two years, it had become difficult to keep a sense of values straight as I began to push aside certain principles that once had mattered the most. Instead, I told myself it would work out, and I half-believed that things would change. I absorbed myself in my home and husband, hoping that by keeping myself busy, the wrinkles in our family's tapestry would flatten themselves out without any attention. When they did not, I persistently tried even harder to ignore them.

Little by little, over the years, bitterness had seeped in as conflicting priorities over concerns had sowed seeds of discontent. Little by little, my soul started to lose ground. At first, I went about daily routines, burying any trace of resentment that my husband worked the evening shift and often on weekends. Given his demanding hours of work, we had more days spent apart than together. More and more, he and I began to pursue separate interests, and I focused on our sons' activities. The emptiness did not go away. I regarded myself as a moral person. After all, Sundays were set aside for worship. I often prayed. I tried to be a good person. *Is that all it takes?* I wondered. My relationship with God had also become clouded, and I felt more and more distant from Him.

Never could I have imagined the ultimate struggle I was

about to face. On the surface, I acknowledged my relationship with God. On a deeper level, however, I was being shaken to the core as I distanced myself and allowed bitterness to set in. Day-to-day I clutched tightly to a dream that was slowly vanishing before my eyes.

I had grown up in a home with unshakable old-fashioned values. Among them was a strong belief that you were bound in a marriage forever. Divorce was never an option. It was like a bad word never to be spoken. If the marriage was imperfect, that, in essence, was a cross to bear.

The day my marriage shattered, our family unit fell apart as well. I had only fooled myself in thinking it shattered in one day. Communication, listening, sharing feelings and concerns honestly and openly, and working together for the sake of the marriage and family had been almost non-existent. Honest and open communication breaks down over time, leading to trouble ahead. If only I had noticed it had broken down before our relationship was in serious, even irreparable, danger.

When I heard my husband speak the words "I don't want to be married anymore," I tried feverishly to put the broken pieces back together again. Despite everything, I had certainly loved him, naively thinking this could never happen to us. My thoughts waxed nostalgic. I ached for us to be a family again, untouched by thoughts of divorce. I waded through the photo albums, where the good times remained unaltered. As if in a state of shock, I grasped at any option that would help us stay together, unwilling at the time to even remotely consider a separation. We began counseling, together at first, then separately, hoping that in the end it would help pull us together.

Day-to-day living took a great deal of effort. My exhausted body and anxious mind kept me awake for hours on end at bedtime. Just getting up each morning and working full-time required a special dose of stamina. I literally forced myself to eat since my weight slipped to a little over one hundred pounds and would have posed health problems had a weight drop persisted.

The mere thought of divorce created overpowering uncertainties and fear. How in the world would I manage on my own, with two sons and a home to take care of? Balancing a checkbook was new to me, as was keeping up with the normal maintenance of a home and yard. The idea of maintaining the car on my own was even more overwhelming. If we were to become divorced, those very stresses would be added to the process.

One thing after another seemed to be falling apart. The turmoil just would not end. When my husband moved into his own apartment, around the time my car was totaled in an accident, I thought if there is a Hell, we were certainly living in it.

It would have been so easy for me to give up by drowning out the wrenching emotions with a bottle of liquor. Anything to numb the pain would have been better than facing the turmoil. Realistically, I knew it would not go away. It would have stayed suppressed, only to surface again and again until I dealt with the feelings and came to terms with some of the underlying issues for which I might have a responsibility.

For months after the first mention of divorce, I tried to handle things on my own, holding on to what I had worked for all those years. I was so stubborn, thinking that I could do it alone. It was a fear of my own making that entrapped and kept me from moving forward. Anyone who has found themselves in a similar situation knows that separation is a time of confusion. It can be a time of anger and pain. For me, the future was unthinkable. I felt as if a mental brick wall had been placed before me and I could not begin to penetrate it beyond that point.

There were stressful days I wondered if God had completely abandoned me. *Where is He in all of this mess? What good could possibly come from the turmoil?*

Bewildered, I moved aimlessly about the house with its reminders of a past stage of my life everywhere. From the extra space in the double closet, to the uncomfortable emptiness of the bedroom, all told me it was no longer the same. I cried at the oddest of times, especially when I heard a favorite oldie on the radio and would remember where my husband and I were the first time we had heard the song. It also happened when a letter directed to him was delivered to our address, and when someone called, asking to speak with him. How could I tell people he no longer lived here? Suddenly, I was beating back the tears.

I was in limbo, searching for answers to what had gone wrong, for what I needed to do, for what I needed to hold on to and what I needed to let go of. Letting go was the hard part. After all, it meant letting go of a familiar identity: wife, mother, homemaker. It meant stepping into the insecurity of an unknown future. *How can I let go of such a big part of my dream?* I wondered. *How can I let go when it had been so hard as a child to say good-bye?* Good-byes are never easy.

My life became an emotional roller coaster, alternating between hopeful days when I felt our marriage might still work out and more doubtful days that left me in the depths of despair. There were frantic calls to the therapist for help in sorting things out. We oscillated between staying together or going our separate ways permanently. A big part of me kept wrestling with God, insisting that this was not the way it was supposed to be.

I found myself distanced from married friends. Being separated and working full-time definitely had an impact on some friendships formed during the marriage. A few close friends remained in touch; most, however, changed and drifted away.

I searched relentlessly for the wisdom to make sound decisions that would affect both my life and that of David and Alan. My prayers slowly began to come from the heart as I earnestly prayed for courage and strength. Months of professional counseling and much prayer had not helped. The decision to divorce became clear. Sitting in the attorney's office in October 1991, I closed my eyes and covered my face with my hands to fight back the tears. I knew that things could not linger as they had.

Filled with a determination to survive, I sought support wherever I could find it. My family pulled together, helping my sons and me in any way they could. Relying on my faith more than ever before, I held tight to the promise that God's goodness would indeed prevail. I had to believe that more than anything.

Some nights the stream of tears would not stop. Alone in my bed, I often felt I could cry forever, tears running down my face on to the pillow until I became too exhausted to cry anymore. At first, my sons were shielded from the tears. In order to protect them, I resisted having them see the anguish and sorrow I felt. It later made more sense that they, too, needed to deal with the situation as much as I in order to begin to heal, in a sense giving themselves permission to express their own thoughts and emotions.

Then one evening, in February 1992, several months after the divorce process had already begun, quite by accident I ran into a family friend I had not seen or heard from in years. As he and I sat down and talked a while, I heard him say, "Kathy, I know of a supportive singles group that meets every Wednesday night at a church, near the center of Glastonbury. Why don't you go? You might find it helpful."

I couldn't make the effort at first. But after a few weeks went by, in light of all I was dealing with, I realized I *had* to do something.

And that was the beginning ...

Chapter 11

God was about to take the struggles and change my life. It began one Wednesday evening with a church ministry focused on the spiritual and emotional growth of single adults of all ages and of many faith backgrounds. The Singles Forum met weekly, without fail, at the First Church of Christ, Congregational on historic Main Street in Glastonbury, where the Reverend Dr. Carl Schultz, Jr. has been pastor since 1968.

Sitting in the church's large social hall full of perhaps one hundred people or more, I sensed the warmth and felt welcomed in, not knowing anyone but a friend I had convinced to attend with me.

At the end of the evening, the minister closed with prayer. The words touched my heart, stunned and overwhelmed me. I *felt* every word with such intensity that it gave me the hope, strength and assurance that I no longer needed to carry my struggles alone. It was as if all the effort of trying to handle everything on my own, on my terms, had been lifted.

His prayer will always stay with me:

In all of your daily living, may you ...

Remember that God is above you watching over you like the Good Shepherd who loves you so much;

Remember that God is below you ready to lift you up when you are feeling weak;

Remember that God is behind you, encouraging you forward when you may want to turn back;

Remember that God is in front of you, calling you forward when you're not sure of the steps ahead;

Remember that God is beside you, holding your hand through whatever it is you are going through; and most of all . . .

Remember that God is within you, within every breath you take, giving you the strength and the courage to go on.

And that makes all the difference in the world. Amen.

Those words became a source of comfort. As unsure as the steps ahead were, there would be no going back to the way things had been.

I returned to The Singles Forum week after week and slowly began to connect with the people there. Its focus was and continues to be on affirming single adults as whole persons. Through a variety of educational programs and formats, including large group discussions, book series, and special musical programs, I felt drawn even more to this weekly group. Rev. Dr. Malcolm Marler, the Associate Pastor and facilitator at the time, supported the volunteer leadership responsible for various activities.

Self-esteem was low so making friends was not easy, but yet I knew it was important. I began to hear how other people there had similar experiences or had gone through similar transitions (not necessarily divorce) in their own lives. Hearing their stories helped me put into perspective what I was dealing with. God's love began to appear through other people.

Week to week, I began to relate more and more to the topics presented — topics on dealing with grief (and divorce certainly is a grieving process), on letting go, on prayer, and on the need to care for oneself. I learned about the importance of forgiveness of others and forgiveness of self. I could not move forward without giving myself permission to let go of the bitterness and stop blaming myself for what had gone wrong.

For the first time in the divorce process, I saw a flicker of light at the end of the tunnel, hope for the future. I began to realize the pain subsiding into steps of growth. In time, I started to heal. The smile slowly started to come back. Slowly, laughter began to feel good again. Things started to fall into place and changes began to take hold.

In October 1992, within only seven months of attending The Singles Forum and already a year into the divorce process, I had built up enough courage to sign up to do a brief meditation before the program for the evening began. It seemed like such a small step, but to me it was the beginning of many more to follow. I have always admired anyone who could captivate an audience with what they had to say. It looked so easy to watch others at the podium. For me, it had always been difficult to get up in front of a group of people. It was not something I could have imagined doing comfortably with confidence. One-on-one conversations were fine. But in a large group setting, I lacked the confidence. The meditations, however, were steps needed for growth. At first, I began my prepared meditation and felt my knees shake as I stood there for the duration of perhaps three to five minutes.

Surely, my face must have shown my nervousness. Certainly, I felt the flush of sudden heat. I realize it was a small step, but it has become much easier to do over time.

The memory of one Thanksgiving eve at the Forum stands out in my mind.

Our group was on its own that particular night. Our new facilitator was away for the holiday and it was an evening of sharing. We encouraged those who were willing to come up to the podium and share what they were grateful for. We asked everyone to bring either a canned or frozen vegetable or something to add to our "Stone Soup". And we asked those who could to bring a food item for a basket I would deliver that evening to a needy family in Glastonbury. The outpouring of items was unbelievable. Although our turnout was on the low side, twenty-five to thirty showed up. I opened for the evening. That meant welcoming everyone in the church social hall with a short introduction of what The Singles Forum is all about, introducing the person for meditation, and doing the announcements before the program began. I was amazed how well it went. When our program began, some people were willing to share stories of what they were grateful for. I started; others followed.

I stood there at the podium, taking it all in. The smile on someone's face, a friendly nod from another in the back row, the intense look on still another; people showing their interest as if to say, "I hear you." When it was time for soup and bread in the church kitchen after the program, we gathered together in prayer. I felt a "oneness" with the others that night I had never experienced before. I realized then that so many had become my friend, each in his or her own way: with their wonderful hugs, a kiss on the cheek, or with a kind word spoken. They had, in time, become my extended family.

Chapter 12

To this day, a card sitting on my bedroom dresser in full view from any point in the room serves as a daily reminder when I awake and when I retire for the night. It was given to me by my sister Mary during the time of my divorce by way of encouragement. The card simply says: "Trust in the Lord with all your heart and lean not on your own understanding." Inside, it continues: "God brought you this far, He won't abandon you now. Trust Him."

Trusting means not being afraid. It means letting go of circumstances, without fear or worry. It means believing that God loves us unconditionally and has a purpose and a plan for our lives.

The process of rebuilding my life and learning to take care of myself had become an exercise in deep reflection. The challenge of a new life was emerging.

The divorce process was ongoing, almost two years of motions, negotiations, and court dates. It was often hard, emotional work, sorting through all the feelings. There are many steps. The first step I have found helpful is the willingness to work through what is going on and the willingness to allow positive changes to take place. Change is never easy.

Keeping a journal had made a big difference to me in sorting out my feelings and thoughts. Expressing them became therapeutic. Quite often in protecting ourselves, we run the risk of becoming unable to withstand the storms of life which arise without warning. It may be serious illness or the death of a family member or someone close to us, or it may be disappointments that alter our lives. It may even be divorce. The very pressures can keep building and building until the stress becomes insurmountable. Frightened, we may not know how we're going to get through. Wanting to pull the covers over our heads seems like an easy way out. However, by ignoring the feelings or denying that they exist, or by stuffing them inside, we run the risk of having our health suffer, both mentally and physically.

Expressing feelings, whatever they are, brings healing and builds strength. By looking within ourselves, we come to know ourselves better. It is often so easy to look back to past mistakes or experiences. It takes awareness and action to change some of the old patterns of behavior or ways of thinking which may need changing. It takes getting to know yourself, knowing who you are independent of the role you take part with family, friends, spouse, or children.

For me, there were, no doubt, occasional setbacks. Of course, I have sometimes reverted to old ways of thinking. The setbacks have become fewer and fewer, however, as new, more grounded ways of dealing with the changes, disappointments and stresses were learned.

A friend often reminded me, "Let Go and Let God." Healing is a step-by-step process that takes time. Taking it one day at a time was often the only way I could get through. The future may have been uncertain, but I needed to learn to trust all over again in a God that will guide, day by day. Scripture tells us that our needs are known to God, who will not forsake us. It is important to remember every concern, every care would be taken care of in the right way, at the right time. We should never give up trying, all the while remembering that

Spring 1951 – Katherine sits on her father's lap on the day of his departure from Yugoslavia to America.

1953 – The old house in Lisnja (Bosnia)

The old church in Lisnja.

April 1953 – Family and friends see Evgenija Oborski and her children off for the United States. Helen and Katherine pose with their Grandmother as she holds Steve.

April 1953 – Evgenija and her children, Helen, Katherine and Steve pose for one last photograph before departing for the United States of America.

May 11, 1953 – Arriving in New York. A new life begins.

1956 – Evgenija Oborski and her children help with yardwork at St. John's Ukrainian Catholic Church in Glastonbury, Connecticut.

September 1984 - Mary and Katherine meet their relatives upon arrival at Belgrade Airport, Yugoslavia.

October 1984 –
Mary and
Katherine ride
into town with
Uncle Vladimir.

October 1984 – It was a long walk from Uncle Vladimir's farm in Bosnia into town.

October 1984 – Katherine and Aunt Katarina and Uncle Vladimir on his farm in Lisnja, standing in front of the wagon which had transported Katherine as a little girl to the train station in 1953.

October 1984 – Stopping for a photograph in Prnjavor, Yugoslavia.

October 1984 – A multitude of icons adorn the altar of the little church in Lisnja.

October 1984 – Cousin Genjo's daughter (second from right) rehearsing with a folk dance group outside of Belgrade, Yugoslavia.

October 1984 - Cousin Genjo and an uncle get ready for a pig roast celebration.

October 1984 – Family, friends, and neighbors gather for food, laughter, and dancing on the evening before Mary and Katherine are to depart for the United States.

God will open doors that need to be opened. People will come into our lives to help us each step of the way.

Over a period of time, weeks and then months, in going back to the journal I kept, it became clear to me that changes had already taken place. I had made progress. Part of the process of healing, I found, has been discovering all over again who I hope to become. It has been important to hold onto how I want to live my life, what values matter the most. I cannot look at some things in exactly the same way. They no longer are the same. Much of the scaffolding of my life has changed. Priorities have shifted. The tendency, therefore, has been to strive for what feels real and important.

What had started as an outlet of writing down feelings in order to move forward, helped me to face the losses and eventually would bring healing. In the process, jotting down those precious particles of my life has fostered a passion for writing.

In striving to find the best place to grow in my spiritual journey, I found myself slowly letting go of a church that had once nurtured me. Now, I was moving toward a different point in my faith journey. It was vital that I keep my spiritual life alive and growing. Having rediscovered the magnitude of God's love, I yearned to know Him on a deeper spiritual level.

As a child, I had heard God often portrayed as someone who was there to punish me. Fear rather than awe and joy became my main emotion in worship. I had faithfully followed my religion, but now as if for the first time, I had begun to see God as a gracious, loving, caring, and compassionate God, ready to accept me as I am.

It became obvious that I needed to change churches. The question I wrestled with was how could I find the peace in making a break away from a church that had been a significant part of most of my life — over forty years in this country? The little Ukrainian Catholic Church had been such a big part of my life ever since my childhood, especially when my father had been involved with so many aspects of it. It had always been a very small community of people where everyone knew everyone else. They helped one another when needed. When someone died, everyone was there. When there was a baptism, everyone was there. Here, I had learned to sing the Slavonic hymns by heart and where I had made my first Holy Communion, where my sons had been baptized shortly after birth, and where they had served as altar boys during Sunday services well into their teen years. Here, I had become involved as Secretary of the Women's Guild and had helped with the dinners and fundraisers. Most of all, here my mother had instilled in me the rich customs and traditions of our faith and culture, traditions that had been passed on to her by her mother and grandmother, traditions I had tried to carry on all those years but had slowly allowed to slip away as we had become more and more Americanized. Sadly but realistically, I knew these were traditions my sons would most likely not continue.

In going back to the little church I had attended all those years, I found myself examining so much. Now the congregation was only a handful of people — perhaps fifteen or sixteen at the most. The number had dwindled each year as the older ones, the founders, died. I was the only one from my large family to have continued there all those years, holding on to the traditions of my childhood.

But it was different now.

The feeling of spiritual fulfillment I used to cling to was gone. The old priest had had a dynamic, charismatic personality and was now retired. The new priest's sermons came across rather empty. Prayers seemed all too repetitious. At the end of the Mass on this particular Sunday morning, even with the warmth of the sun filtering through the stained glass windows, I felt unfilled spiritually. *What would I do?*

As hard as it had been sometimes, I have learned to wait patiently for answers and direction.

One morning I was reading a book, *Embraced By The Light* by Betty J. Eadie. A friend had given it to me as a birthday gift. A passage seemed to stand out. It was as if the paragraph had been written just for me, the message mine alone. I read that each of us is at a different level of spiritual development and understanding:

> *Each person is therefore prepared for a different level of spiritual knowledge. ... People in one religion may not have a complete understanding ...while in that religion. But that religion is used as a stepping stone to further knowledge. Each church fulfills spiritual needs that perhaps others cannot fill. ...As an individual raises his level of understanding about God and his own eternal progress, he might feel discontented with the teachings of his present church and seek a different philosophy or religion to fill the void. When this occurs, he has reached another level of understanding and will long for further truth and knowledge, and for another opportunity to grow. At every step of the way, these new opportunities to learn will be given.*

It became another answer to prayer. In my searching, I had found an answer. All I needed was to allow myself quiet time to be receptive to receive the messages, to receive the answers. They have often come unexpectedly through someone I happened to come in contact with, or through a stranger or chance meeting, or even through a book or lyrics of music. They may have seemed like coincidences, but I believe they were not.

For almost a year, I had attended several different churches of varied denominations in the Glastonbury area. What I found is how comfortable I had become by attending the services of First Church, where I originally started with The Singles Forum. I sensed the warmth of the people upon entering the large double doors of the historical church and later as I became introduced to them at coffee hour after the service. It has been a church open to all people, with a Christian emphasis on loving one another in a nonjudgmental way. There were and continues to be countless opportunities to become involved for both adults and children: an excellent Christian education program, youth fellowship groups, several choirs, Special Visitors and Stephen Ministers, and a Care Team ministry. It has been a place that centers on the needs of others, both within the congregation and reaching indirectly beyond.

I felt as if I was coming home.

Chapter 13

Days grew into weeks, weeks into months, one year into the second until the divorce became final. The legal ordeal was over on January 21, 1993. In the process, I had learned about co-dependency, lack of self-confidence and low self-esteem. I had learned as well about setting boundaries, being assertive, and recognizing where my true responsibilities lie.

Lessons of the past became doors of opportunities opening up.

I grasped the opportunity when it presented itself to become involved in a women's empowerment group held once a month. The facilitator's experience as a holistic counselor, consultant, and seminar leader became very helpful as it allowed me the opportunity to visualize new possibilities for the future, new ways to enrich my life as a single person. Our time together often helped to clear a direction, one built on strength. As a result of my association with the ten women involved in the group, all of us having gone through one type of transition or another, special friendships have become formed.

I began to discover qualities within that had laid dormant. A restored semblance of where I was going began to take hold, shaping my interest in the endless possibilities of ways to reach out and help others.

Through a newspaper article, I learned about a training program for the Literacy Volunteers of America, English As

A Second Language. How fitting it seemed, a parallel of my own past. After going through the necessary training, my first assignment was to help two sisters, Irene and Elisabeth, newly arrived from Romania. We met once a week, two hours at a time, for about a year. What is remarkable is that we learned from each other. They benefited by a better understanding of the English language. My life, in turn, became enriched by hearing their story. They, too, had left their country and family behind.

Another opportunity, just as rewarding, opened up for me to become actively involved in a confidential, one-on-one caring ministry within First Church called the Stephen Ministry. This ministry focuses on care given to those experiencing various life transitions: loss due to illness, death, divorce, employment issues, and much more. It was a program I had taken advantage of in the early stages of working through the process of divorce. During that time of need, I had been fortunate to have had assigned to me a woman trained in the caring ministry. Her continued presence and willingness to listen to my then otherwise bottled-up concerns had helped to lessen the stress I had experienced. She had also instilled hope for the future for my sons and me, something that had been crucially vital for us. The Stephen Ministry program certainly made a difference in my life and it now opened doors for me to become involved in return, by being a part of a team working together to provide compassionate care to those in need.

My life was beginning to fall into place.

Chapter 14

Things went along for another three years with a sense of renewed purpose and direction.

It was one of those mornings, on a hot and humid July morning in 1996 that I awakened from a dream startled. Something was wrong. As soon as I was fully awake, I was able to realize I was hemorrhaging heavily.

"Oh, no!" I screamed as I put one foot on the floor and attempted to get out of bed. The scream had been loud enough to awaken David from the next room and as he ran to the doorway, he stopped abruptly.

"Mom! What's wrong?" he exclaimed as he stood motionless in the doorway long enough to realize what was happening. A spasm of fear was written all over his face. Before I could even utter a word, he exclaimed, "You look awful! We're getting you to the hospital — now!" He knew from his experience of working at the local hospital while taking college courses, that if I didn't get immediate attention, I would be in serious trouble. Without giving me even a moment to change the soiled clothing, he took my arm and managed to help me into his car.

The drive to the hospital never seemed so distant before. Only three miles away, today it felt endless.

Waiting in the Emergency Room, I thought back to a few months earlier. Bloating had been a daily reality. Fatigue as well. I had been to more doctors than I cared to remember, with more than one visit to the Emergency Room. Still there had been no concrete answers for the cause. Ever the optimist, I thought a common outpatient procedure would take care of the problems I had been experiencing.

"Katherine — I need to take some blood work," the nurse says to me gently stirring me out of my reverie. A young woman about David's age squeezed between the bed and wall in the cubicle area and prepared to draw the necessary blood. Shortly, a doctor came in, took the information for the paperwork needed, and performed a pelvic examination. A few minutes later, another doctor showed up and did exactly the same. I was being poked, prodded and examined more than I cared to be. Where were the answers? Finally, a third doctor, the gynecologist on call, took over. *Why did it have to take three doctors?* When he was done with the examination, I was whisked away by stretcher to Radiology for an ultrasound.

Directly beyond the elevator, the doorway of Radiology loomed before me like an entrance to uncertainty. I took a deep breath and said a silent prayer: *Dear God, how I wish this would be a simple procedure. Let it be so, I pray. Let it be nothing more than that, Lord, and I will be home again. Please help me. Amen.*

The x-ray technician immediately began the procedure and questioned whether I felt any discomfort. My head lay flat on the stretcher, making it impossible for me to see the screen. All I could do was to watch her face as her hands guided the probe back and forth across my stomach. When another technician came in and stood watching the monitor, I feared there was more to all of what was happening.

After reviewing the results of the ultrasound, the doctor and nurse returned to my cubicle and stood beside the bed. Their faces already told me something was wrong. Their expressions said it all well before I heard the doctor speak the words.

"We need to talk," the doctor began, as if trying to lessen the impact of his words. It was obvious, however, from the tone of his voice, that the situation was serious.

"The results from the ultrasound have come back ..." he stopped mid-sentence, then continued, "... and it shows what appears to be a large pelvic mass. We suspect it to be an ovarian malignancy."

"A tumor?" I muttered, after awkward silence. The doctor nodded affirmatively and hesitantly, as if preparing himself for an outburst of hysteria at any moment from me.

Had I heard clearly? A pelvic mass? *What could he be talking about? I'm much too young!* I took a deep breath and tried to fight back the tears. *God, what am I going to do if it's true?* Still in shock, I felt every muscle in my body tighten. *No, it can't be true. I'm too young for something like this to happen.* A frantic feeling followed as the nurse took a step closer and reached for my hand. She knew I needed some reassurance or maybe support in case I felt apart. A sense of urgency in the doctor's voice elicted more fear from me.

"We need to schedule you for exploratory surgery tomorrow." This news was too hard for me to grasp. Still fighting back the tears, I turned my head away, completely burying it in the bed pillow.

Chilling thoughts raced through my head faster than I could process them. They were saying that in all probability the growth was malignant. *Cancer. How in the world could this be? Cancer that happens to other people. Not me. Breast cancer that took Mama's life only thirteen years earlier.* My mind races on. *Thyroid cancer that had touched my sister Mary's life shortly after our trip to Yugoslavia, a cancer which required her to have surgery and treatment. Thank God, she is still alive today.*

Never facing it fully before, I realize how much my mother's cancer and death had haunted me. I had taken strides to stay as healthy as possible. Pap smears, mammograms, and x-rays were normal procedures I had taken in the past to alleviate the risk. I had wanted to be free from this dreaded disease, and had tried to do everything I possibly could in order to avoid what my mother had faced or what Mary had gone through. I had taken up running and had even run the five-mile Manchester road race two years in a row. There had been a balance in my life of work, family, friends, and fun times. *So*, I ask myself, *how could this be?*

My anxiety soon swelled completely out of proportion. I began thinking the worst — that cancer might take my life and strip me from seeing Alan graduate from high school next summer and David graduate from college. *No, I can't think such thoughts. I have to believe everything will work out. It just has to.*

"I'm not sure I can handle this," I confessed to the nurse by the side of my bed. Overwhelmed, disoriented and confused, my mind was under siege.

The nurse, still holding my hand, looked directly into my face and quietly asked, "Is there someone you would like me to call for you?" Unable to answer her, I turned my head away instead. I felt totally unprepared to face this reality. The doctor and nurse left me alone in the room to face a hurdle unlike any other I had ever faced.

Feeling powerless and alone, I began sobbing, terrified by the uncertainties ahead. Ovarian cancer is an aggressive disease, often referred to as the deadliest of all gynecological cancers. From the very start, it often has few symptoms. That explained the bloating and tiredness I had felt for months. As the cancer advances, there is often abdominal pain as it spreads to vital organs.

Completely drained, both emotionally and physically, I now needed time to rest. Any decision to have exploratory surgery or transfer to a larger hospital would just have to wait.

The next morning, my brother Steve arrived, quickly dispelling my qualms. "Have a second opinion, Kath," he recommended. There was no time to waste and he was willing make the necessary arrangements. That afternoon, I transferred to St. Francis Hospital in Hartford.

After a second opinion and after extensive tests are performed, I underwent five hours of surgery the following day. Waking in my room following the operation, I was gagging on a tube that ran through my nose and esophagus into my abdomen. Every time I tried to swallow, I felt I was going to choke. I became panic-struck from the sight of intravenous tubes, catheters, and monitors all around the bed.

My son Alan, alarmed over my condition, remained with me throughout the first night. Every now and then, waking from my drugged stage of sleep, I would glance over at the blurred image of him stretched out on the recliner by my bed. Now seventeen, he was ready to enter his senior year of high school. The divorce had hit him hard. He had kept a tight rein on his feelings for a long time. If he had shared them with his friends, I was not aware of it. He had been nearly twelve — such a vulnerable age — when my marriage began to fall apart. Tough years of peer pressure and academics then faced him. It seemed to have finally caught up with him in his sophomore year. We had talked more openly by then — about the divorce, about how different our lives were because of it.

Now, as I looked over at him beside my hospital bed, I

felt proud of his progress and prayed that I would be alive to see him graduate from high school and David graduate from college the following summer.

Like a breath of fresh air, day by day, I began to feel less groggy. Flowers arrived. Then cards. The response from my Singles Forum friends touched me deeply. One card read:

Last night at Singles Forum, we learned you were in the hospital. So you are in all our hearts and minds and prayers. I pray for wisdom and knowledge for your doctors and nurses. For you, I pray for healing and peace. We all look forward to seeing you in the near future. Know that you are loved. Love, Ocean.

And another card read:

I'm sorry to hear of all you've been through. I am praying for your complete recovery and that each day will bring new strength. May God give you peace. Pat.

And from my family, a beautiful card read:

Dear Sister: We wish we could take your pain away. We wish difficult things wouldn't happen to good people. What we can do is say we feel your hurts, your pains. You are in our prayers. You are loved very much and we need you. So, rest. Please don't worry. Heal and come home to us. Whatever you need, Sister, we will always be there.

Only a week after being discharged, during a follow-up visit to the surgeon's office, I am informed of the pathology report. I will need a minimum of four chemotherapy treatments as a precautionary measure. With all the new drugs for chemotherapy on the market, I felt confident that I would not have to lose my hair. What would I have to face? I learned words I never knew existed — Carboplatin, Toxol, Decadron, and more. The oncologist, however, he informed me that the particular drugs given for treatment of ovarian cancer, unfortunately, would result in hair loss for me. I felt devastated beyond words. The thought of losing my hair disturbed me more than anything else.

My youngest sister, Trish, came to my rescue.

"Come on, Sister," she said. "We've got a hairdresser to meet." By way of preparation, she and I made a trip to the hair salon shortly before chemotherapy treatments. To make it less traumatic, my hair was cut from shoulder length to the shortest cut possible without shaving it completely. In the days that followed, an appointment was confirmed to pick out a wig beforehand.

My first treatment began four weeks after surgery, in early September. Covering several hours, if I had to stand up, the bag suspended from the IV and a metal box attached to it that regulated the flow of chemicals went with me. The premeds finally lulled me into a drowsy state of mind, making it impossible for me to read the book I had brought with me. Rather than fight the drowsiness, I tried to relax and allow the treatment do what it was intended to do.

Within three weeks of receiving my first treatment, clumps of hair began to fall out at even the slightest touch, until the last trace of hair became lost in the rush of water and gathered at the bottom of the shower drain. There was nothing else for me to do but cry.

Rest and recovery were essential. The time I had for recuperation before going back to work would allow me to read more than ever. I found myself needing to learn everything I could about the future of my body: ovarian cancer, the drugs that are used for treatments, the prognosis, the importance of regular exercise, good nutrition and daily vitamin supplements. Keeping a healthy, positive attitude was just as crucial. In reading Dr. Bernie Siegel's book, *Love, Medicine and Miracles*, I decided I needed to become the "exceptional cancer patient" he highlighted in his book.

Blood work was monitored on a weekly basis between the scheduled appointments. I learned that when the white blood count becomes low, the chances of infection are greater. At first my fingertips became numb, then my toes. It became hard to button. My eyelashes went, then my eyebrows. These are all so-called normal side effects, the result of neuropathy. The effects of a chemotherapy treatment hit me especially hard a few days later. I experienced aching and fatigue, and the insomnia became frustrating since I often awakened two or three times during the night.

Returning to work during this time of treatments became extremely emotional. I had no choice but to keep working, primarily for financial reasons, as I struggled to pay the mortgage and make ends meet. When it became difficult to work, if I tired or became sad with the process of loss, I found the need to release the emotions. I could not hide them, nor could I make them go away. I became sensitive to the smiles and cheerfulness around me. The people I worked with meant well, as they tried hard to lift spirits. A point came, though, when I could not hold a happy face. I had to make them understand I appreciated their concern, but I needed to acknowledge the loss in the process of dealing with it. In the end, they were understanding and supportive. I felt like a tremendous burden had been lifted, to be allowed to release the emotions in the process.

I needed to let go of the fears, the wave of anxiety that was always ready to take hold. I needed to trust once again that God was going to get me through as I recuperated, as I faced changes due to hair loss and side effects, worked full-time, and continued with chemotherapy treatments.

My family encouraged me to do whatever felt comfortable when I began to complain about wearing a cap to cover the baldness and as I tired of the wig. Their main concern was, of course, that I regain my health. David's and Alan's friends often visited, giving me a tremendous boost with their friendly hellos and hugs. My sense of peace became rooted in the smiles on their faces as they walked in through the front door.

Treatments followed every three weeks until November, just before Thanksgiving.

In order to avoid foreclosure, I placed my home up for sale; but even in a good real estate market, with the holidays approaching, it took a lot of effort on our part to keep it in good showing condition in order to sell it more quickly. My sons and I began to gather cardboard boxes in an attempt to begin the arduous task of packing. Boxes quickly filled with photographs in frames and albums, along with the usual accumulation of a household of over twenty years. As hard as my sons and I tried, the whole ordeal began to take its toll. There were too many changes occurring in too short a time span.

Each passing day, though, I became mindful of the blessings in my life. I began to feel grateful for the unbelievable outpouring of love, the showering of concern from so many loving people in my life — my brothers, sisters, nieces, nephews, aunts, cousins, friends, co-workers, and church family. Their cards, telephone calls, gifts of flowers or food brought to the home, and frequent visits often overwhelmed me with gratitude. They encouraged and gave me hope — good, caring people opening their hearts, offering their support and their earnest prayers.

As sure as the peace that surfaced, I knew God was watching over me. For many years, He had been preparing me for what I was now dealing with. I had been through tough times before and I had learned along the way to let go of circumstances enough to allow Him to take over. I had done my part; He would do the rest. The strength to endure had been provided before. I was now certain it would always be there.

I am glad to be alive. No, it is much more than that. I *love* being alive. It is different now. I love following my life's passionate impulses as if for the first time, rediscovering all the feelings, grasping all the joys, all the experiences, savoring precious moments I may have so often taken for granted.

Six months after chemotherapy treatments ended, I felt as if a tremendous weight had been lifted. No more trips to the Gray Cancer Center in Hartford. No more Emergency Room visits in the middle of the night. No more wig and no more hats to wear. That in itself made my spirit soar. Just as the oncologist had predicted, faint strands of hair had begun to surface within six weeks of the last treatment. Now, instead of a short stubble look, there was no end to the welcomed tight curls covering my head.

It dawned on me that I had in time become accustomed to the solitude of single life. Who would have ever thought it possible? The aloneness that had once felt uncomfortable, even unbearable and unthinkable, no longer bothered me. I even embraced the physical and emotional solitude, knowing that there is a significant difference between being alone and being lonely.

My days begin like any other, with a steaming cup of freshly brewed coffee brought back to bed. I am delighted in the luxury of feeling the softness of the sheets, caught up in the ultimate comfort of being back in bed a few minutes longer. It is essential for me to carve out a few precious minutes to sit and be still. Unlike before when constant demands needed to be met, when the frazzled mind often raced at a dizzying pace with the numbing effects of a hectic life, making note of yet more things to do to fill up my day-to-day calendar, I now opted for a more relaxed approach to life. Practice and discipline have their rewards.

Up until March 1997, I had been the homeowner of a seven-room house with almost an acre of land behind the Globe Hollow Reservoir in Manchester, one of the nicest locations in town. In the gardens there, I had often found refuge as I flung myself into yearly planting and transplanting. Home now was a simple, but comfortable, 1,000 square foot, two-bedroom unit overlooking the Buckland Hills Mall, where the perennial gardens had become replaced at least temporarily with hanging flower pots on a small balcony instead.

I dream a wide-eyed dream ... of continued good health ... and blessings of close family ties and special friendships ... of a home nestled behind a white picket fence, only minutes from the center of town ... and of combing the country roads, stopping at old barns filled with treasures.

There is another dream, a more pressing dream. It is time ... time to put the pieces together ... time to go back to Ellis Island.

Chapter 15

Wednesday, May 21, 1997. I had circled the date on the calendar in bright red, three times over.

As the early morning sunshine filtered through the lace panel curtains of my bedroom windows, flooding the room with a profusion of light, I sensed the day would be like no other.

Even before I got out of bed, an exuberant burst of energy, impossible to tame, filled my body from head to toe. It was a jubilant edge of fresh vitality that takes over, quite like the pulsating energy I had often felt when I danced, my feet moving furiously to the beat of a cajun two-step, or like the adrenaline rush of a foot-stomping, head-turning spin of an old-fashioned polka.

This was the day I had planned for these past few months.

I went through my mental list of must-have's: keys, cash, and a light jacket since the days of mid-May were rather unpredictable. The weather forecast called for a warming trend by the end of the day, with temperatures predicted to reach into the 60's. *But weather forecasts have been known to be wrong before. Better to be safe than sorry. Bring the jacket.*

I dug deep into my purse a second time, fumbling to find the worn key chain. *Better find the tickets,* I reminded myself as I continued to search inside my purse. Above all else, I could not forget the tickets.

Everything feels wonderful. In my eyes, the world was wonderful ... my life was wonderful. After an excruciating twelve months that had eaten up all available accumulated sick days and vacation days for illness and chemotherapy treatments, it was a great relief to leave all that behind me.

Walking through the hallway filled with a wall gallery of family photographs worn by age and use, now silent testimony to the past, I glanced out the window to see a picture-perfect glorious blue sky mixed with billowy puffs of white clouds. It could have been a torrential downpour. It could have been bleak and dreary as thunderstorms had threatened each day of the prior weeks of spring, enough so to bring the umbrella along wherever I went. Instead, there is the penetrating warmth of the early morning sun as it touches my face.

Exhilarated, I quickened my pace, locked the door to my apartment, and walked to my car, passing early morning commuters on their way to work. I had to pick up Helen, who lives in the neighborhood next to mine.

"Do you have the tickets?" Helen said rather apprehensively, before positioning herself comfortably in my car and wrapping the seatbelt around her waist. I must have gazed straight at her, taken aback somewhat. How could she even think I'd forget them? Certainly not today.

Allowing ample time for travel, we arrived in the municipal parking lot well before the tour bus was scheduled to leave for New York. Delayed somewhat by the constant flow of traffic entering the city from Connecticut, our bus arrived at Battery Park a few hours later. It was already 10:00 a.m., and there was no time to waste. As we got off the bus, Helen and I fell into step with the others and took our place near the end of the line of tourists.

As I stood in the crisp morning air, its freshness undeniably awakening my senses, ready to board the ferry across the Upper Bay, a stark realization came over me. *I have put off taking this trip for over forty years. Why? And, why now?*

The Statue of Liberty, clearly visible beyond the chain link fence I came to rest against, stood as a grand figure in the background with Ellis Island just as impressive only a half mile to its right. They have stood as gateways for millions of immigrants in the past, and continue to stand as symbols of beauty and freedom today.

Set against the backdrop of the Manhattan skyline, hundreds of people from every race and culture huddle three or four across, crushed into the mid-week crowd. At first glance, some appear intently serious as if momentarily swept away in a swirl of deep emotions, their eyes glazed with a faraway look. Each face in this tapestry of nationalities held a story to tell, as surely as I have mine.

The brochure I held in my hand said it all. The words of a poem written in 1883 by Emma Lazarus almost jumped off the page ... *"Give me your tired, your poor, your huddled masses yearning to breathe free ...."* Those words had drawn waves of immigrants escaping persecution, poverty, or famine from their homeland. They had arrived often with meager belongings, full of a renewed spirit and full of dreams. Generation after generation, they had come seeking a better life, passing on legacies from grandparents to parents to children. Those words brought to mind my own past.

As I retraced my steps from forty-four years earlier, I could only guess what my feelings would be. Would I feel the mystique of deja vu there? Would the large hall still hold the chill of the past? Would the voices of the tourists resemble the echoes of the immigrants? Could the tile on the floor still hold the awe and wonder of all the people whose feet had walked its length?

I could only imagine what it would be like. The buildings had since been meticulously restored from their previous state of disrepair after years of being abandoned. With extensive repair, the historic site had reopened to the public first in 1976 until the island closed again in 1984 and then reopened a second time in September 1990. Thousands of people have since passed through its museum and theater, attracted to the many displays of historic artifacts, all in search of some connection with their ancestors and ethnic backgrounds. Some have diligently searched the Wall of Honor along Ellis Island's seawall for evidence of the name of an ancestor that would bind them to their own family roots and link grandparents to parents and to themselves.

Helen and I, however, remembered the landmark as it had been a year before the doors closed to immigrants for the very last time in November of 1954.

Instinctively, my eyes met the first ferry closely approaching the harbor, and in a moment of sheer panic, Helen and I knew we needed to take action. In an instant she and I politely maneuvered our way through the line, weaving in and out very quickly in an attempt to be among the first to board. We knew full well that we were cutting in line — not something we usually did. Feeling rather embarrassed yet holding back laughter, she and I found ourselves beside the chain link fence ahead of the group we had arrived with, looking back at them.

Upon boarding, and as we made our way up to the open platform, it was impossible to suppress our pent-up emotions. The excitement was far too great to remain seated in one place for too long. She and I found our way through the crowd to a spot with the best panoramic view and stood there against the railing. Suddenly the engine blared a loud jolting noise and the ferry broke away from the dock, leaving the towering city skyline behind us. We were on our way!

With cameras in hand, Helen and I took one long look at each other. She stopped to fix the collar of my jacket, standing it straight against my neck to protect it from the wind. She has always been kind, gentle in everything she does. My big sister, she has always thought of me. No wonder we were taking this trip together.

"Here goes," she said, suddenly taking a deep breath and then looking across the water as if a memory of long ago had been stirred and awakened. I turned to her and noticed tears beginning to form in the corner of her eyes. In the next breath I heard her say, "I know I'm going to cry."

"It's okay," I assured her, putting my arm around her as if to give her permission to do so. Nothing could have more aptly expressed my own feelings. I was surely going to do the same. "It's okay."

"Do you remember? ... over there ..." She extended her arm, pointing to the huge Verrazano Narrows Bridge with its looped cables connecting Brooklyn with Staten Island, leading out to the Atlantic Ocean. "That's where our boat came through that day ... under that bridge. Remember?" Her eyes squinted from the brightness of the sun peering through the lifting clouds.

I gave a quick nod: yes. My recollection was vivid. I remembered arriving as a passenger on the *CONTE BIAN-CAMANO*, a name that had stayed with me primarily because of the photographs that filled an album at home.

Helen began to speak again. "Can you believe it! We're finally going back after all these years!"

"I can't believe it either! I can't believe it's taken us this long," I replied with a keen sense of bewilderment.

Shifting my place on deck once more for a clearer, unobstructed view, I suddenly lost my train of thought and stopped in awe as if momentarily paralyzed. My eyes were drawn first to the massive Statue of Liberty, which loomed as the ferry turned the corner and allowed a handful of passengers to disembark. While Helen and I wanted to equally embrace the timeless attractions, we had to make a choice as to whether we should get off and split up our limited time between the two sites or focus only on one. Given the short amount of time we had available, we decided to proceed straight on to Ellis Island.

As the ferry moved on, my gaze suddenly turned from the Statue and the haze of memories toward the breathtaking view of the American flag set on its pole on the edge of Ellis Island. It was enormous in size as it unfurled in the breeze, with the backdrop of the Manhattan skyline. I stood motionless, my vision fixated on the brilliance of the red, white, and blue of the stars and stripes as it unleashed a harmony of pride and gratitude. Overwhelmed with such deep feelings, I was awestruck by the majestic power it had over me. I sensed that same highly potent combination of pride and patriotism I had often felt in the past when hearing *The Stars and Stripes* and watching Alan, decked out in his striking red and black Manchester High School band uniform, playing the drums with the marching band in the Memorial Day parade. Or when I had heard a rendition of the national anthem sung loudly and boldly in an overfilled ice hockey rink while David stood as co-captain in the forward line during season playoffs in his senior year.

Standing on the ferry with Helen by my side, I could not erase from my mind how different life would have been if I were living in Bosnia today. It was even much more than that.

If fate had been different, I wondered, *would I be here today? Would I be alive?* Given the turmoil that has continued to plague the country once known as Yugoslavia, given the conflict that has been called the bloodiest "ethnic cleansing" war in Europe since World War II, would I have been one of the countless victims of the horror?

The constant barrage of newspaper headlines and magazine articles continuously related stories of the unbelievable events that have taken place in that area. Countless innocent men, women, and children have lost their lives in the destruction over the years. Even I had watched television newscasts with full-color visions of grenades exploding, burning villages, charred buildings, and the look of devastation as tired faces have dug mass gravesites. Even I had become desensitized to the daily loss of lives and unfathomable human cruelty beyond comprehension. Waiting for news of the outcome of peace talks, even I had prayed when all efforts of peace talks appeared futile. I had prayed that the NATO air strikes would inevitably bring peace.

The headlines still speak to me in a very personal way. Not too long ago, I learned of a cousin, her husband, and two sons who found it necessary to evacuate their home in Tuzla, just outside of Sarajevo. They had been forced to join other refugees as the regular, thunderous crashing sound of artillery gunfire had become a certain threat. Her last letter had emphasized the overwhelming, ongoing fear they felt for their lives. And then the letters stopped being delivered.

Tensions had begun in 1991, although the ethnic hatred had been brewing for centuries, growing from the seeds of fear and ignorance that had steadily been eroding the foundation of the country. It was the Serbian guerrilla forces who waged war against the militia in Croatia, including Tuzla. In another letter from yet another cousin living outside Belgrade, I learned that the Serbian forces continued to move further North into the town of Vukovar, where an elderly uncle [my father's brother] and his family remained pinned to their home yet were miraculously saved from a direct hit as they witnessed a nearby church they attended burned to the ground. Severe bombardment, destruction, and hunger, as well as the unspeakable brutality forced on its people, took its toll in the siege on the town until Vukovar surrendered. Now, it is hard to imagine how life can ever be restored to the area where, in 1984, I sat with my uncle in that beautiful church in Vukovar when I had visited the country for the first time.

With the touch of a finger, I wiped the flow of tears from my eyes, ever more aware of the power of the words in the brochure in my hand: *"Give me your tired, your poor, your huddled masses yearning to breathe free."*

It was too difficult for me to remember what it was like living in the outskirts of Yugoslavia. There was a time where memory most certainly failed me. The memories were not forgotten, however; merely pushed to the farthest recesses of my heart in order to be protected from their painful barbs. Rekindling thoughts of what it had been like as a young child saying good-bye to my father and hearing him say I could not go with him would have been too devastating and as painful as hearing him say: "I'll send for you later."

Surely now, after all those years, after all that has happened, after a life characterized by a series of one loss after another, through one change after another, surely now I could look back and recognize that throughout it all, from the beginning in a small village in Bosnia to where I now stood, somehow I have come through it all with my heart and soul intact. For forty-four years, my dream of a better life has remained alive, although bruised and battered by sorrows. Somehow, I have become stronger. *What has brought me to this point? What has brought me through each tug of the soul leading up to this point in time?*

I realize that I had needed to learn and re-learn certain valuable lessons, even while resisting some, before I could begin to understand the basis for my personal security and strength or before I could begin to appreciate the growth I have experienced emotionally and spiritually. Some lessons I had needed to learn before I could appreciate the significant impact a decision to immigrate to this country had made in my life. It was a life-changing choice, first made by my father. How courageous my mother must have been to follow two years later, not able to speak a word of English, a single worn suitcase in hand and three small children by her side.

Their choices profoundly affected how I lived my life, favorably and unfavorably, despite my own best efforts at times. It is useless to dwell on the unfavorable, on the "should-have's, what-if's, or if-only's." It is more important, no, crucial, to have learned from the events and to move forward. Regardless of the past, there is the promise of another opportunity, hope for another day and the opportunity to begin over.

I cannot help but think of what it means for me to live in this country. From an early age, a very impressionable age, America has sheltered me and has provided conveniences and freedoms I would not have otherwise ever known. For that, I will forever be most deeply grateful.

Epilogue

I retreat to Bailey Island, Maine, for a weekend away.

The weather is undeniably brisk for Columbus Day. I position myself on a layer of rock forming a slope, with rows of weathered cottages behind me and the panorama of the ocean before me. In the distance another island, barely visible, appears as clusters of clouds once blocking its view fade away. Yesterday's warm sunshine has been replaced with the cool freshness of morning and the thrashing of whitecaps on the ocean water. There is nothing to do but listen to the sounds — swirls of seagulls hovering overhead then diving and swooping up again, the pounding of the waves against the rocks, and the sounds of the moaning wind telling me winter is on its way.

The end of the year 2000 is fast approaching and a new millennium is about to begin. Alan is now three years into serving in the military, stationed at the U. S. Naval Air Base in Brunswick, Maine, and living on the island. David is on his own and continues to work in the medical field. I have seen them both grow into maturity as they now envision their own dreams. They, too, will have a story to tell.

I have experienced one of the best weekends away from home. Surely I have needed to take time for unhurried pleasures that stir my soul to be still and appreciate life more fully. I have loved walking the narrow main road of Bailey Island, inhaling the fresh ocean air on one side and looking beyond at the beauty of Mackerel Cove, filled with bobbing lobster traps and fishing boats coming in and going out. I have stood on the deck with my morning coffee, watching the sun come into view, moved by the radiance of the beauty around me.

Instinctively, I have learned to brush aside any "why?" questions that had once lingered on my mind, questions I had often asked when disappointments and stressful events surfaced and I had found myself tugging at my faith. I have learned along the way that when I am able to let go of the fears and work through the situations, love enters in, bringing with it serenity. Gratitude begins to open the door ever so slightly to an emerging joy, leaving me with an awareness of the simple treasures life holds.

I realize only too well how fragile life is. Anyone who has lived with a life-threatening illness or disability or has seen a loved one face death or has been overtaken with grief can relate to just how precious each day becomes.

I realize there are no guarantees that life will hold only happiness. It can be good, yes. It can also bring difficulties along the way. The journey may not always be smooth and easy. It is helpful to take its bits and pieces and gather strength to keep going. There is an important promise to remember, however, *in all times.* I believe we can carry it with us wherever we go, through every circumstance, in every situation. We can remember we are never alone.

Our lifelong dreams, our day-to-day events, remind us to trust that God can provide us with all that we need, in His time, in His way. Our smallest cares, our deepest hurts, our moments of sadness, and our moments of joy — He is part of them all.

As the weekend on the island comes to an end, it has been in those early moments of dawn as light streaks across the sky that I could not let the day begin unnoticed without celebrating it.

Before darkness takes hold, nothing compares to watching the sun plummet to the horizon, splashing a rainbow of miraculous color all across the sky. I have witnessed the most beautiful of sunsets: a sky saturated with pinks, purples, and blues. It has been enough to take my breath away. It is in those moments that there is heartfelt peace.

Surely, Heaven must be like this.

About the Author

Known for her penchant for sensitivity and compassion, Katherine Ciolkosz (K.Ciolkosz@worldnet.att.net) focuses on volunteer work catered to the needs of others. Her background includes training as a Literacy of America volunteer (English as a Second Language) as well as hospice work in the Greater Hartford area. She is an active member of First Church of Christ, Congregational in Glastonbury, Connecticut, where she has served on the Steering Committee of The Singles Forum. She also serves as a Stephen Minister and Stephen Leader since 1995, and more recently has taken on a leadership role in implementing Care Teams as part of the church's caring ministries. The last three years have added the rewards and challenges of being a Youth Advisor at the junior high school level.

At the heart of her life are her two sons, David Ciolkosz and Alan Ciolkosz, their dog Odee, and her large family of two brothers, three sisters, and many nieces and nephews.

She recently has returned to live in Glastonbury, only miles from where she began her life in this country in 1953.

To contact the author:
Katherine Ciolkosz
1 Hillside Avenue
Rocky Hill, CT 06067